THE COMPLETE LIBRARY SKILLS
Grade 4

By
Linda Turrell

Cover and Inside Illustrations by
Darcy Myers

Publishers
T.S. Denison & Co., Inc.
Minneapolis, Minnesota 55431

Standard Book Number: 513-02211-1
The Complete Library Skills—Grade 4
Copyright © 1994 by T.S. Denison & Co., Inc.
9601 Newton Avenue South
Minneapolis, Minnesota 55431
Printed in the USA

TABLE OF CONTENTS

WELCOMING FOURTH GRADERS TO THE LIBRARY

As you get older you will be spending more and more time in the library working on projects and reports and looking up information. Although you will be taught about many of the basic resources and systems of the library, you will probably always have some questions about how to find something that you are looking for. This is why librarians work in the library – to help you!

Below is a list of things to remember when you work with librarians:

1. Introduce yourself to the librarian and get to know them. They are working with most all the children in the school and they will probably need help remembering your name.

2. Often there are many people who need the librarian's help, be patient and quietly wait your turn.

3. When you ask your question, speak clearly and give the important details needed for the librarian to help you.

4. When the librarian is through helping you, be sure to say thank you for the time and guidance he or she gave you. You might even write the librarian a short note saying how your project or report (or book!) turned out.

BOOK CARE RULES - REVIEW

Libraries are places where people go not only to check out books, but also to study or read quietly. Speak softly.

Remember that when you check out books you are only borrowing them. People will use them again after you so you need to treat them with respect.
- Never write in books.
- Keep books away from pets and small children.

Do not re-shelve books. It is very easy to accidentally put a book back in the wrong place; let the librarians re-shelve the books you do not want.

Return books when they are due, other people may want to check them out. (You could make a large note to yourself to remind you when your books are due back at the library.)

If you are using a library where you need a library card, be sure you keep it in a safe place and do not lose it. (Do not give your card to a friend to use – you are responsible for any books checked out on your card.)

LIBRARY CITIZENSHIP – IDEAS FOR TEACHERS/LIBRARIANS

Children will have likely already heard many of the rules on the preceding page, but you will probably want to refresh their memories. Here are some ideas:

1. Ask the children to recall important library rules. Using a blackboard or chart paper, write down the rules as they are given. Some of the reponses can be combined, others may be broken down into two rules.

2. Test each rule by asking the children why there should be such a rule.

3. Have each class member draw a poster illustrating an aspect of library etiquette. hang the posters in the classroom or library.

4. Finally, after all library rules have been discussed, distribute the "Library Citizenship" reproducible (page 7) and have the children come up with as many rules as they can remember about the proper use of the library.

CITIZENSHIP IN THE LIBRARY

These are rules we follow in our school so that everyone can enjoy the library.

1. _____

_____

_____

2. _____

_____

_____

3. _____

_____

_____

4. _____

_____

5. _____

_____

6. _____

_____

7. _____

_____

AUTHOR'S NAMES

When using the library, we often find that an author's last name appears before the first name, with a comma in between. This format is used in the card catalog, indexes, and bibliographies. Ordering people by their last name is the easiest because so many people have the same first name. If you ask your teacher, he or she will probably say that you and your classmates are listed last name first on the student records.

If you wanted to look up the author Scott Corbett, you would look in the "C" card catalog drawer (author section) and look under "Corbett." When you found the card you would see **Corbett, Scott** at the top of the card. This sounds simple, but some authors have tricky names like Maud Hart Lovelace, Hans Christian Andersen, Dick King-Smith, Gerald McDermott, and Judith St. George.

Here are some rules to follow when looking up author's names or people's names in the subject section of the card:

1. Authors that have either two last names or a middle name and a last name should always be alphabetized with their very last name.

   So Maud Hart Lovelace would appear: **Lovelace, Maud Hart** and Hans Christian Andersen would appear: **Andersen, Hans Christian**.

2. Authors also occasionally go by their first two initials. The same rule applies:

   E.M. Almedingen becomes **Almedingen, E.M.** and A.H. Drummond becomes **Drummond, A.H.**

3. When authors hyphenate their last name, like Antonio Jimenez-Landi, the whole hyphenated name is put ahead of the first name: **Jimenez-Landi, Antonio**.

4. Last names with "St.," as in St. George and "Mc" names like McDermott present a slightly different problem that occurs when you are trying to look up these types of names in the card catalog. When you look up any name that starts with "St." you must think of it as SAINT and look it up starting in the Sa's rather than the St's.

   Similarly, if you are looking up a last name beginning with "Mc" (there are many of them!) you must think of it as MAC and look it up starting in the Mac's rather than the Mc's.

NAME _____

AUTHOR NAMES ACTIVITY

Write your first, middle, and last name.

_____

Someday you may be an author, Write your name the way it would appear in the library card catalog.

_____ , _____ ,_____

Write these author's names with the last name first.
(Don't forget the comma)

Jamie Gilson _____

Tasha Tudor _____

Laura Ingalls Wilder _____

Yoshiko Uchida _____

Joan W. Blos_____

Trina Schart Hyman _____

Donald J. Sobol _____

C.S. Lewis_____

Ezra Jack Keats _____

Gyo Fujikawa _____

Madeline L'Engle _____

A.A. Milne _____

Lois Lenski_____

AUTHOR CARD FORMAT
AND ALPHABETIZING

Look at the author cards below. For each card, write the author's name on the line the way it would appear in the card catalog (last name, first name). Remember the rules!

After you have written out all the author's names, put the cards in alphabetical order by numbering the boxes in the circles provided.

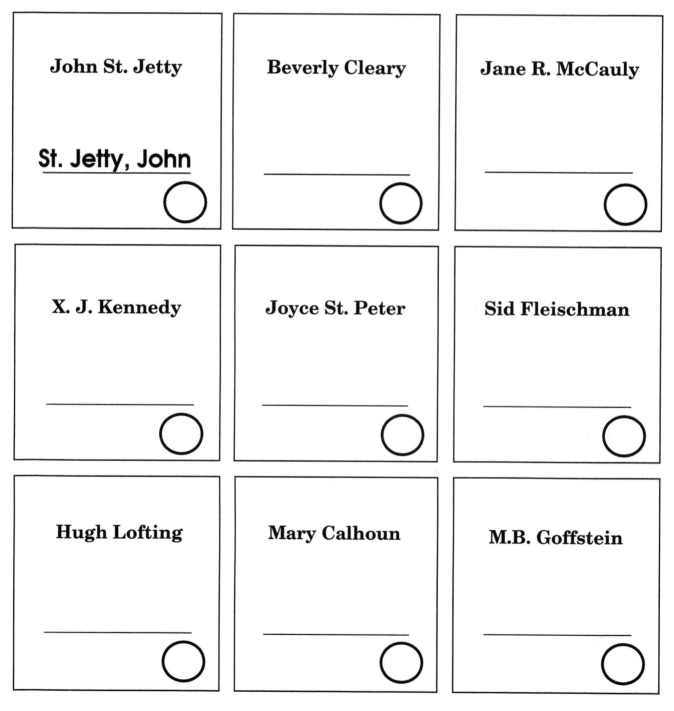

John St. Jetty

St. Jetty, John ⃝

Beverly Cleary

_____ ⃝

Jane R. McCauly

_____ ⃝

X. J. Kennedy

_____ ⃝

Joyce St. Peter

_____ ⃝

Sid Fleischman

_____ ⃝

Hugh Lofting

_____ ⃝

Mary Calhoun

_____ ⃝

M.B. Goffstein

_____ ⃝

FICTION OR NONFICTION?

Do you know the difference between fiction and nonfiction? In order to find books quickly and easily, you need to know the difference between these two categories. Your library has an entire section of books that are fiction. They are shelved together. You will find them easily because their call numbers are in alphabetical order. You can find what you need by looking for the letter F and then the first two letters of the author's last name. The letter F stands for "fiction" — books that have stories which are made-up or imaginary.

Nonfiction books are also grouped in one section of the library. They are grouped first in number order and then alphabetically by the first two letters of the author's last name.

Nonfiction books are based on facts. They tell you about people, places, and how to make or do things. They give you a lot of information. Nonfiction books can tell you about travel, history, science, or biography. These are just a few subjects of nonfiction books.

By knowing where the nonfiction and fiction sections are in your library, you will be able to search for books more effectively and easily.

IS IT FICTION OR NONFICTION?

Read each description. Is it fiction or nonfiction?

1. *The Chicken and the Dragon* by Arthur C. Feather. This is the story of a dragon who helps a chicken remember his way home.

   _____

2. *The Planets* by Peter Starlight. This book describes the planets in our solar system. Descriptions and pictures of each planet are included.

   _____

3. *Explorers Go to America* by James Boat. This book gives the routes the explorers took to America. Maps and illustrations are given.

   _____

4. *Pinky, the French Poodle* by James Poof-Poof. This is the story of a French Poodle with pink fur.

   _____

5. *Dinosaurs of Long Ago* by Peter Tail. This book tells the type of dinosaurs that lived long ago.

   _____

6. *Dogs and Their Owners* by Roger Leash. This book describes the types of ways to train your dog.

   _____

7. *How to Start Your Aquarium* by Peter Fish. This book tells what to buy and how to put it together.

   _____

8. *Sports Legends* by Alvin Bat. This book describes the lives of famous sports stars.

   _____

9. *Flower Designs* by Hilda Vase. This book tells how to arrange flowers for special occasions.

   _____

10. *Hamsters! Hamsters! Hamsters!* by Roger Pellet. This book tells how to train and care for your hamster.

    _____

IS IT FICTION OR NONFICTION?

Read each description. Is it fiction or nonfiction?

1. *The Sneaker Mystery* by Arthur Shoestring. This is just one more story by Arthur in his mystery series. In this story, a sneaker has gold shoelaces. Where is the rest of the hidden treasure? Arthur solves the case.

   _____

2. *Snakes in Your Backyard* by James John Slink. This a complete book of common snakes. Pictures of each snake are included.

   _____

3. *The Day of the Rabbit* by John Carrot. This is the story of a lonely rabbit's adventure with a small boy.

   _____

4. *The Spelling Mystery* by Linda Vowel. Mr. Haley's Friday spelling test mysteriously disappears from his desk.

   _____

5. *Rabbits, Gerbils, and Hamsters* by Richard Fur. This book gives step-by-step pet care instructions.

   _____

6. *Dinosaurs and Fossils* by Richard Bones. This book describes what dinosaur fossils look like and how they were discovered.

   _____

7. *Dragons and Other Beasts* by James Firebreath. This book tells tall tales about strange creatures.

   _____

8. *Learning French* by Linda Language. This book tells how to learn French.

   _____

9. *The Great Turtle Race,* by Edward Shell, tells the story of a small town's day-long turtle race.

   _____

10. *The Softball Rule Book* by John Base. This book gives all the official rules of softball.

   _____

IS IT FICTION OR NONFICTION?

Read each description. Is it fiction or nonfiction?

1. *Your Fish Tank* by Peter C. Fish. This book gives helpful hints and facts for setting up your own fish tank. An index and table of contents are included.

   _____

2. *The History of New Jersey* by William States. This is the complete history of New Jersey.

   _____

3. *The Green Parrot* by Sally T. Feather. This is the story of a green parrot. The parrot meets a mouse who wants cheese.

   _____

4. *Snakes* by Richard Slink. This is a science book that tells interesting bits of information about snakes.

   _____

5. *Famous Explorers* by Christine Wander. This book tells about the lives of famous explorers.

   _____

6. *The Mystery of the Orange Canary* by Edward Spyglass. Mr. Spyglass solves another baffling mystery.

   _____

7. *Famous Biographies* by C.W. Writer. The book tells the life stories of ten famous people.

   _____

8. *Birds* by John T. Sparrow. This book describes the nesting habits of fifty common birds.

   _____

9. *Cookies for Sale* by Charles Chip, is a story of a young boy who makes $500 selling cookies at his sidewalk booth.

   _____

10. *Roller Skates!* by Mary Wheel. This is the story of six-year-old Allison's first pair of skates.

   _____

NAME _____

IS IT FICTION OR NONFICTION?

Read each description. Is it fiction or nonfiction?

1. *The Blue Shoe Mystery* by Sandy Sandal. This is a spy story. The mystery is never solved.

   _____

2. *Trees* by Lea Leaf. This book tells about all the different types of trees found in North America.

   _____

3. *Your Country* by James Johnson. This book gives many facts about the fifty states.

   _____

4. *Explorers of the New World* by Captain Olson. This book tells the true stories of famous explorers.

   _____

5. *A Puppy for Hire* by Bowser T. Dog. This book tells the many mysterious adventures of Barker, the undercover agent. Barker plays the role of a puppy but he is really a dog.

   _____

6. *Tenzi* by Willis Polly. This book tells the adventures of Tenzi, a green parrot, who escapes from the pet shop.

   _____

7. *Pets: How to Care for Them* by Robert C. Vet. This book gives helpful and practical tips about animal care.

   _____

8. *Tiffany, the French Poodle* by Sally C. White. This is the story of Tiffany and her new friends. Just one more book in a series of fine dog stories.

   _____

9. *Horses!* by Richard Saddle. This book tells the history of the horse in America.

   _____

10. *The Case of the Missing Key* by Roger Lock. This is the story of a key that fits a hidden treasure chest.

   _____

ARRANGEMENT OF FICTION

Fiction books are shelved in an area separate from the nonfiction books. A book that is fiction is a made-up or imaginary story. These types of books are all arranged alphabetically by the author's last name. The fiction call number is made from the two letters of the author's last name with an "F" (for "fiction") above these two letters.

To find a fiction book:

- First go to the fiction section of the library.

- Then find the correct shelf by searching alphabetically for the author's last name.

- After finding the author's last name, find the book by looking for the title.

NAME _____

ARRANGING FICTION BOOKS

First make the call numbers for the following books and write them on the blank to the right of the title. Arrange the book titles on the make-believe bookshelf as they should be arranged on the shelf in the library. The first one has been done for you.

The Great Gilly Hopkins by Katherine Paterson	**Pa**
Dear Mr. Henshaw by Beverly Cleary	_____
Dump Days by Jerry Spinelli	_____
The Friendship by Mildred Taylor	_____
Fudge-a-Mania by Judy Blume	_____
Doctor De Soto by William Steig	_____
Homer Price by Robert McCloskey	_____
Like Jake and Me by Mavis Jukes	_____
Sarah, Plain and Tall by Patricia MacLachlan	_____
The Whipping Boy by Sid Fleischman	_____
The Cabin Faced West by Jean Fritz	_____
A Fine White Dust by Cynthia Rylant	_____

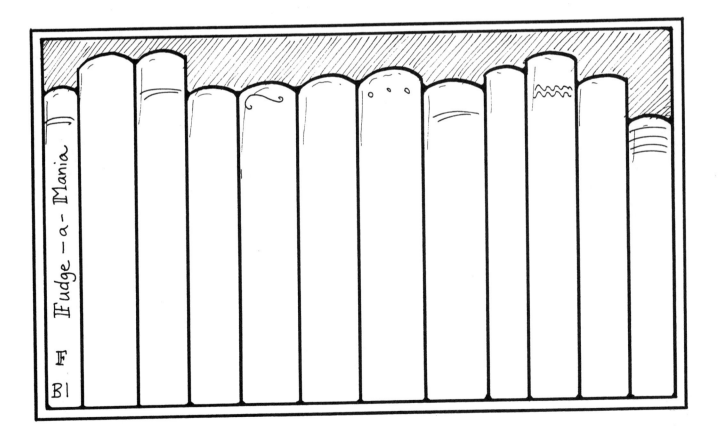

ARRANGING FICTION BOOKS

Books are arranged on the shelf in alphabetical order by the author's last name. Underline the author's last name. To arrange the book titles in an alphabetical list by the author's last name, print the author's last name, then a comma, then the first name, a period and then the book's title. The first one has been done for you.

Quentin Corn by Mary Stolz
Paddington's Storybook by Micheal Bond
Strawberry Girl by Lois Lenski
Billy and the Indian Cave by C.W. Anderson
Mary Poppins by P.L. Travers
Farmer Boy by Laura Ingalls Wilder
On the Far Side of the Mountain by Jean Craighead George
Afternoon of the Elves by Janet Taylor Lisle
Martin's Mice by Dick King-Smith

1. **Andersen, C.W.   Billy and the Indian Cave**

2. _____

3. _____

4. _____

5. _____

6. _____

7. _____

8. _____

9. _____

10. _____

ARRANGING FICTION BOOKS

First make the call numbers for the following books and write them on the blank to the right of the title. Arrange the book titles on the make-believe bookshelf as they should be arranged on the shelf in the library. The first one has been done for you.

1. *The Trumpet of the Swan* by E.B. White   **F**
                                                                 Wh

2. *The Wreck of the Zephr* by Chris Van Allsburg   _____

3. *Ginger Pye* by Eleanor Estes   _____

4. *Saying Good-Bye to Grandma* by Jane Resh Thomas _____

5. *Henry* by Nina Bawden   _____

6. *Five Children & It* by E. Nesbit   _____

7. *The War Party* by William O. Steele   _____

8. *The Midnight Fox* by Betsy Byars   _____

9. *The House at Pooh Corner* by A.A. Milne   _____

10. *Island Boy* by Barbara Cooney   _____

Now, using the shelf below, put the call numbers you made in the order they would appear in the library. The first one has been done for you.

F Ba									

ARRANGEMENT OF NONFICTION

Nonfiction books are found in their own section of the library, separate from the fiction books. Since nonfiction books are books with true facts about many different topics, these are classified and numbered according the type of information that is in the book. In addition to being numbered, nonfiction books also have the first two letters of the author's last name beneath the number.

The number by itself is known as a **class number**. This number tells you the subject section (or topic) of the books. Class numbers in the library range from the 000s to the 999s.

The **nonfiction call number**, which is made up of both the class number and the first two letters of the author's last name, will give you a certain book's exact "address" in the library.

218	920	722.4	218 Fe	920 Br	722.4 Li
671.8	542.89	175.30	671.8 Je	542.89 Ma	175.30 Yo

CLASS NUMBERS
(subjects)

CALL NUMBERS
("addresses")

The arrangement of nonfiction in a library is similar to the arrangement of food in a grocery store. The same types of foods are classified into aisles like books are classified into 200s, 300s, 400s, etc. Like books, foods are narrowed down further within the rows. For example, you would likely find rolls, buns, and loaves of bread in the same aisle, just as you would find all the language books (French, Latin, Spanish, etc.) in the 400's section of the library. **Books about the same subject are placed together.** If you think of class numbers like aisles in a grocery store this might help you understand nonfiction arrangement more clearly.

ARRANGEMENT OF
NONFICTION BOOKS

Arrange these class numbers on the make-believe books as they are arranged in the science section of the library.

550	530	590	510	500
520	598	560	580	570

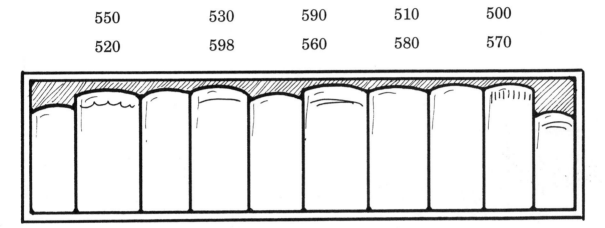

A book's complete call number includes the first two letters of the author's last name. Arrange the books in the correct order on the shelf.

570	510	500	550	520
Mo	Nu	Wh	Br	Ze

500	580	530	520	590
Je	He	At	Fl	Si

ARRANGING NONFICTION SHELVES

Look at the shelves below. Each row is out of order and the books need to be rearranged in the correct order. Remember that if the numbers are the same, you need to order the books by the first two letters of the author's last name.

430 So	450 Ju	480 Iv	420 Le	460 Va	410 Te	490 Ri	400 Ch

291 Dr	563 Qu	744 Em	022 Vi	904 Ul	390 Ph	459 Du	888 Ye

371 Th	354 Bl	359 Fr	347 Ze	354 De	349 Ce	359 Ma	354 Su

761 Ab	743 Ho	761 Ge	720 Ne	766 Tu	720 No	761 Kl	698 Pe

ARRANGEMENT OF NONFICTION WITH DECIMALS

Many times call numbers have decimal points. This is just another way of further dividing sections (or topics). Let's look at some call numbers in one section only. For example, the 910 section of the library is classified "Geography & Travel." Within the 910 section, the 917s are classified as "Geography & Travel in North America."

917.1 CANADA – Geography & Travel

917.2 MEXICO – Geography & Travel

917.3 UNITED STATES – Geography & Travel

As you can see, the decimal points are used here to divide areas of the North America Geography & Travel section into smaller subsections.

When you look for a nonfiction book, the call number will always have letters with the number, but to better understand the decimal numbering system, practice ordering the following class number groups (call letters without numbers) from lowest to highest.

(Complete this activity with the children using the blackboard or a transparency on an overhead projector.)

1. 201.4 _____
   515.6 _____
   108.9 _____
   786.6 _____
   053.2 _____

2. 324.1 _____
   329.8 _____
   321.2 _____
   327.7 _____
   322.4 _____

3. 878.2 _____
   878.9 _____
   878.1 _____
   878.4 _____
   878.7 _____

4. 631.4 _____
   043.2 _____
   629.9 _____
   631.5 _____
   941.8 _____

5. 774.7 _____
   629.3 _____
   774.1 _____
   629.5 _____
   628.9 _____

6. 302.79 _____
   451.84 _____
   302.23 _____
   302.66 _____
   451.82 _____

PUTTING NONFICTION CALL NUMBERS IN ORDER

A *call number* found on the spine of a nonfiction book tells you where you can find that book in the library. The number tells you what section of the library holds the book and the letters (first two letters of the author's last name) tell you who wrote the book.

Example: *All About Butterflies* by John Wing has a call number of 595.7 Wi.

Many times call numbers will have a decimal point. This is just another way of further dividing the section. Let's look at some call numbers in one section only.

401	Which comes first?
412	Answer: 401
468	
424 Ar	Which comes first?
429 Nu	Answer: 421 We
421 We	
453 Mo	Which comes first?
453 Du	Answer: 453 Du
453 Li	
400.6 Bo	Which comes first?
400.5 Be	Answer: 400.3 Bi
400.3 Bi	
400.7 Tr	Which comes first?
400.7 Wa	Answer: 400.7 Ba
400.7 Ba	

Remember: Call numbers are arranged in number order. Then numbers following the point are put in order. Finally the letters of the author's name are put in order.

NAME _____

NONFICTION CALL NUMBERS— DEWEY NUMBERS

A call number is found on the spine of a book, a book pocket, and a book card. You will also find a call number on the upper left corner of a catalog card.

In order to use the nonfiction section of the library you will need to know how books that have call numbers with decimal points and letters are shelved.

All numbers are arranged in number order. Then the numbers following the decimal point are put in order. Lastly, the letters of the author's name are put in order.

Example: 365.1   Which comes first?
365.2   Answer 365.1

Example: 365.3 Ab   Which comes first?
365.3 Tr   Answer: 365.3 Ab

Put these call numbers in order:

1. 564.2 Ar _____
560.2 Ba _____
545.2 Ar _____
510.2 Tr _____
507.2 Ar _____

2. 610.3 Ab _____
607.3 Ar _____
604.3 An _____
605.3 Ro _____
603.3 Ab _____

3. 864.1 Fe _____
854.8 Vi _____
857.6 Ro _____
861.3 Tu _____
852.1 Lc _____

4. 305.1 Ar _____
306.1 Ta _____
301.5 Ro _____
298.3 Ui _____
300.4 Kr _____

NAME _____

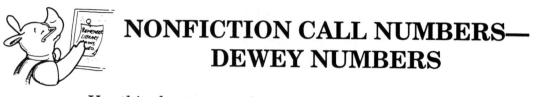

NONFICTION CALL NUMBERS— DEWEY NUMBERS

Use this sheet to practice putting nonfiction call numbers in order.

1. 507.4 Gh _____
    501.8 Ye _____
    513.3 Pl _____
    567.6 Vo _____
    591.4 Em _____

2. 610.5 Ab _____
    607.4 St _____
    601.3 Dr _____
    601.7 Ke _____
    609.5 Hu _____

3. 910.5 Ba _____
    917.9 Ro _____
    898.1 Lu _____
    917.4 Po _____
    625.5 Iv _____

4. 410.5 Tr _____
    398.4 Iv _____
    410.1 Za _____
    410.3 Ri _____
    467.5 Le _____

5. 917.6 Cl _____
    914.6 Ta _____
    917.1 Hi _____
    920.3 Os _____
    914.8 Br _____

6. 153.1 Ye _____
    143.6 Ni _____
    153.9 Je _____
    147.9 Wo _____
    143.9 Kl _____

NONFICTION CALL NUMBERS—
DEWEY NUMBERS

Use this sheet to practice putting nonfiction call numbers in order.

1. 021.4 Bl _____

    593.7 St _____

    241.9 Ur _____

    021.4 Mi _____

    593.6 El _____

2. 658.2 Je _____

    642.1 Am _____

    658.9 Ne _____

    642.4 Zh _____

    658.2 Fr _____

3. 723.1 Di _____

    722.9 Le _____

    450.6 Or _____

    723.1 De _____

    722.3 Ph _____

4. 848.8 Me _____

    848.9 Cr _____

    848.9 Ch _____

    848.2 Th _____

    848.8 Mi _____

5. 051.2 Ni _____

    037.7 Da _____

    129.4 Wh _____

    051.2 Ne _____

    113.9 Ru _____

6. 391.6 Pr _____

    298.4 Ot _____

    391.8 Fi _____

    298.4 Os _____

    391.6 Po _____

NONFICTION CALL NUMBERS— DEWEY NUMBERS

Use this sheet to practice putting nonfiction call numbers in order.

305.2 Ab	1. _____	560.1 Ad	1. _____	401.2 Qu	1. _____
301.2 No	2. _____	560.4 Tr	2. _____	401.4 Tr	2. _____
306.2 Ra	3. _____	560.7 Sh	3. _____	401.6 Br	3. _____
303.3 Ta	4. _____	560.1 Uv	4. _____	402.8 Fe	4. _____
301.3 Li	5. _____	560.8 Pr	5. _____	401.9 Ho	5. _____
301.1 Ta	6. _____	560.3 Ea	6. _____	402.1 My	6. _____
312.5 Ta	7. _____	560.6 Ca	7. _____	401.3 Mc	7. _____
310.4 Ta	8. _____	560.4 Po	8. _____	402.5 He	8. _____
307.4 Sh	9. _____	560.8 Zo	9. _____	401.7 Gl	9. _____
309.1 Sh	10. _____	560.5 Yo	10. _____	402.3 Ho	10. _____

NAME _____

PUTTING CALL NUMBERS IN ORDER
OVERVIEW

It is important to know how to find the book you need. One way to do this is to be able to put Dewey Call Numbers in order. Put these call numbers in order.

301.5 Ab	1. _____	910.5 Ba	1. _____
210.5 An	2. _____	317.4 Ga	2. _____
973.5 Tr	3. _____	419.5 Bi	3. _____
817.5 Bi	4. _____	910.4 Ba	4. _____
607.4 Go	5. _____	607.5 Si	5. _____
398.4 Ba	6. _____	317.4 Ba	6. _____
510.6 Ta	7. _____	419.4 Ba	7. _____
398.4 Br	8. _____	510.5 Tr	8. _____
398.4 Bi	9. _____	498.5 Ha	9. _____
510.5 Ba	10. _____	510.5 Br	10. _____

THE CARD CATALOG

All of the cards found in the card catalog are arranged in alphabetical order. On the outside of the drawer in the catalog are the letters found in that drawer. These are the guide letters. A card catalog looks similar to this:

A - B	H - J	P - R
C - E	K - L	S - T
F - G	M - O	U - Z

(Recreate this illustration of the card catalog drawers on the blackboard or chart paper as you explain what is in the card catalog drawers.)

In the drawer marked A - B you will find all the cards beginning with A or B. The other drawers contain the cards for all the letters marked on the outside and for all the letters that come in between. If you know the title, author or subject of the book you want, the next step is to find the correct drawer.

AUTHOR CARD

Author cards are put in alphabetical order by the author's last name. If you wanted the book *Black and White* by David Macauly, look under Macauly, David.

TITLE CARD

Title cards are arranged alphabetically by the first word of the title, unless that word is "A," "An," or "The." Then they are put in order by using the second word. For example, if you were looking for the book called A Light In The Attic, look under "L" for Light.

SUBJECT CARD

Sometimes you want a book about a particular subject. You can find these books by looking for a subject card. For example, if you wanted a book about snakes, look in the drawer containing the "S" cards for the word SNAKE. Subject cards look different because the subject is typed in capital letters across the top.

THE CARD CATALOG – Authors

A - B	H - J	P - R
C - E	K - L	S - T
F - G	M - O	U - Z

Look for Author Cards

In which drawer will you find the cards for these authors?

1. Jack Prelutsky   _____

2. Mitsumasa Anno   _____

3. Ingri D'Aulaire   _____

4. Robert Quackenbush   _____

5. John Gaskin   _____

6. Rachel Isadora   _____

7. David Weisner   _____

8. Shel Silverstein   _____

9. Patricia C. McKissack   _____

10. Myra Cohn Livingston   _____

THE CARD CATALOG – Titles

A - B	H - J	P - R
C - E	K - L	S - T
F - G	M - O	U - Z

Look for Title Cards

In which drawer will you find the cards for these titles?

1. *Stuart Little* _____

2. *Number the Stars* _____

3. *Pippi Longstocking* _____

4. *Lincoln: A Photobiography* _____

5. *The Adventures of Pinocchio* _____

6. *The Incredible Journey* _____

7. *The Cricket in Times Square* _____

8. *The Lion, the Witch and the Wardrobe* _____

9. *Charlie and the Chocolate Factory* _____

10. *Maniac Magee* _____

THE CARD CATALOG – Subjects

A - B	H - J	P - R
C - E	K - L	S - T
F - G	M - O	U - Z

Look for Subject Cards

In which drawer will you find the cards for these subjects?

1. CHINA   _____

2. WEATHER   _____

3. SPACE   _____

4. PIONEER LIFE - STORIES   _____

5. GERMANY - FOLK TALES   _____

6. CHRISTMAS - POETRY   _____

7. MYSTERY - STORIES   _____

8. LIONS - STORIES   _____

9. DOGS - STORIES   _____

10. EXPERIMENTS - SCIENTIFIC _____

THE CARD CATALOG – Overview

A - B	H - J	P - R
C - E	K - L	S - T
F - G	M - O	U - Z

In which drawer will you find the cards for these authors, titles, and subjects?

1. _____ A Book by Peggy Parish

2. _____ *Charlotte's Web*

3. _____ VOLCANOES

4. _____ A book by Louis Sachar

5. _____ FLOODS

6. _____ A book by Sheila Hanamaka

7. _____ *The Book of Eagles*

8. _____ Painting Faces

9. _____ *Mrs. Piggle Wiggle*

10. _____ A book by Anthony Browne

11. _____ *Alice in Wonderland*

12. _____ *These Happy Golden Years*

13. _____ *Presidents*

14. _____ AFRICA - ANIMALS

15. _____ MYTHS

16. _____ A book by A. A. Milne

17. _____ *Amelia Bedelia*

18. _____ ELECTRICITY

19. _____ *Aldo Peanut Butter*

20. _____ A book by Lee Ames

WHICH CARD DO I WANT?

You may understand what a card catalog box is. But how do you decide what part of the card catalog to use? There are three parts to the card catalog. The subject, author, and title. When do you use the author section? the title section? the subject section?

First, you must decide what kind of information you already have. Do you know the author's name or the title of the book? If not, do you know the subject of the book? What information do you have?

For example, let's say that you are looking for a book about rocks. Do you know the author's name or the title of the book? The answer to both of these questions is no. But you do know the subject: rocks. So you would check the subject part of the catalog, under "R."

Let's say you need a book called *The Story of Rocks*. Do you know the author's name? the subject? You have the subject but you have more detailed information. You know the title. Check the title section of the card catalog, under "S."

Let's say you need a book written by James Johnson. Do you know the title or the subject? No. But you do know the author's name. Check the author's part of the card catalog, under "J" (for Johnson).

NAME _____

THE CARD CATALOG – Review

A - B	H - J	P - R
C - E	K - L	S - T
F - G	M - O	U - Z

Which kind of card (author - title - subject) will you find the following books?
In which drawer would you find the card?

	Kind of card	Drawer

1. A card for the book, *Rumpelstiltskin* _____ _____

2. Cards to tell you where you can find books about WEATHER _____ _____

3. A card for the book, *Tales of a Fourth Grade Nothing* _____ _____

4. Cards that tell you about books by Jean De Brunhoff _____ _____

5. A card for the book, *Cats Are Cats* _____ _____

6. Cards that tell you where to find books about PRESIDENTS _____ _____

7. A card for the book, *Wayside School is Falling Down* _____ _____

8. Cards that tell you where to find books about THANKSGIVING _____ _____

9. A card for the book, *The Kid in the Red Jacket* _____ _____

10. Cards that tell you about books by James Marshall _____ _____

WHAT CATALOG CARD DO YOU NEED?

You can find the information you need more quickly if you know what part of the card catalog to check.

For example: You need a book about spiders.
Do you need an author, subject, or title card?
See subject card—SPIDERS.

Read each situation. What card do you need? Write "author," "title," or "subject." (You do not need to find the actual answers to these questions.)

1. _____ How many books about sailing are in the library?

2. _____ Is there any information about Christopher Columbus in the book *The Explorers*?

3. _____ How many books written by A.A. Milne are in the library?

4. _____ Who is the publisher of *The Very Hungry Caterpillar*?

5. _____ What is the copyright date of *Tigers*?

6. _____ Your teacher assigned a report on colonial life. Are there any books on colonial life in the library?

7. _____ Are there any books written by Charlotte Zolotow in the library?

8. _____ You plan to bake cookies for a school party, but you do not have a good recipe. Where do you look?

9. _____ You need a picture of the coast of Spain for your report. Where do you look?

10. _____ You would like to learn a few French words. Your friend says *Learning French* is a good book. Where do you look?

11. _____ Your pet gerbil is not looking well. What can you do? Where do you look?

12. _____ Does your library have any books by E.B. White?

WHAT CATALOG CARD DO YOU NEED?

You can find the information you need more quickly if you know what part of the card catalog to check.

For example: You need a book about Abraham Lincoln.
Do you need an author, subject, or title card?
See subject card—ABRAHAM LINCOLN.

Read each situation. What card do you need? Write "author," "title," or "subject." (You do not need to find the actual answers to these questions.)

1. _____ Is there any information about cowboys in your library? Where do you look?

2. _____ You need a picture of an ant colony for your science report cover. Where do you look?

3. _____ Is there any information about cyclones in *What's the Weather*?

4. _____ How many books written by Judy Blume are in the library?

5. _____ Who is the publisher of *The History of New Jersey*?

6. _____ Your teacher assigned a report about the planets. Are there at least 25 books about the planets?

7. _____ Are there any books written by Leo Lionni in the library?

8. _____ Your hobby is baseball. Are there any books in the library about baseball?

9. _____ How many books in the library are written by Dr. Seuss?

10. _____ You collect stamps. Are there any books about stamp-collecting in the library?

11. _____ Who is the publisher of *Whales*?

12. _____ How many books written by Beatrix Potter are there in the library?

NAME _____

FIND THAT SUBJECT
IN THE CARD CATALOG

Read each situation. What subject would you look under in the card catalog?

1. _____ You need a good mystery story for your next book report.

2. _____ What was life like for the dinosaur?

3. _____ You need to know how to fix your skateboard.

4. _____ You need to know the rules of baseball before you sign up for the team.

5. _____ How do butterflies protect themselves in nature?

6. _____ You are constructing a poster for a contest about bicycle safety.

7. _____ You are making a kite for the Spring Fair at school.

8. _____ You need to identify six rocks for a science report.

9. _____ You need a picture of Christopher Columbus' ship for a report cover.

10. _____ You need to know how the planets are positioned in the solar system. Name two subjects.

_____

11. _____ You are trying to find a good recipe for a cookie contest. Name two subjects.

_____

12. _____ You are looking for a drawing of astronauts who went into space. Name two subjects.

_____

THE CARD CATALOG – Review

```
( ) 597          ( )  FISH
     Br           ( )   Brewster, Bernice


                  ( )  Discovering freshwater fish: Illus. by
                  ( )  Vanda Baginska


                  ( )  Bookwright Press   ( )  1988


        46 p                 illus.


Individual chapters are used to describe aspects of freshwater
fish; such as how they breathe, what they eat, reproduction,
enemies, and fish as pets.
```

Find the following parts of the card.

1. Author _____

2. Illustrator _____

3. Publisher _____

4. Title _____

5. Call Number _____

6. Copyright Date _____

7. Subject _____

AUTHOR - TITLE - SUBJECT CARDS

(a)

```
796    FOOTBALL
Ma     Madden, John
              The First Book of Football.  Crown
       1988
```

(b)

```
F
Va     VansAllsburg, Chris
       Two Bad Ants.  Houghton   1988
```

(c)

```
F      The Fourth Grade Discovery Club
Bo     Bogard, Larry, Illus. by Richard  Lauter
              The Fourth Grade Discovery Club.  Delacorte
       1989
```

Answer the following questions.

1. What kind of catalog card is each of the above?

   (a) _____ (b) _____ (c) _____

2. What would the call number be for each of these books?

   (a) _____ (b) _____ (c) _____

3. What is the author's last name for each of these books?

   (a) _____ (b) _____ (c) _____

4. What is the title for each of these books?

   (a) _____

   (b) _____

   (c) _____

5. What is the copyright date for each of these books?

   (a)_____ (b) _____ (c) _____

6. Give the name of the publisher for each of these books.

   (a)_____ (b) _____ (c) _____

COMPARING CATALOG CARDS

It is important to know how to get research information by choosing the correct catalog cards. If you know how to do this your searching time can be reduced. For example, let's say that you are writing a report about the latest developments in space research. Look at the following two catalog cards.

Parker, Lin

The history of space

Space Press, 1976

210 p. illus.

Explains the history of the space program.

James, Edward

Space exploring

Space Press, 1993

510 p. illus.

Explains the latest developments in the space program.

Which card (book) would be the best research resource to help you find out about the latest developments in space? Answer: *Space Exploring*, 1993. What piece of information on the card helps you? The copyright date. A book with the copyright date of 1993 will give you more accurate information than the book with the 1976 copyright date.

COMPARING FICTION CATALOG CARDS

```
F      Butler, Peter
Bu        The purple squirrel. Nuttree Press, 1987.
          28 p. Illus.
          A purple squirrel visits and eats all the plums in
          the refrigerator.
```

```
F      Peters, Robert
Pe        The alligator in the refrigerator
          Crocodile Press, 1988.
          32 p. Illus.
          An alligator in the refrigerator greets a small child.
```

Look at both cards. Answer these questions.

1. _____ Who is the author of *The Purple Squirrel*?

2. _____ Who is the author of *The Alligator in the Refrigerator*?

3. _____ Which book is illustrated?

4. _____ Which book has more pages?

5. _____ Which book was published first?

6. _____ Which book was published by **Nuttree Press**?

7. _____ Which book is fiction?

8. _____ Which book has a call number **F** ?
                                                        Pe

9. What is *The Purple Squirrel* about? _____

    _____

10. What is Robert Peters' story about? _____

    _____

NAME _____

COMPARING FICTION CATALOG CARDS

> F   Peterson, Albert
> Pe   The case of the missing pelican.
>   Pelican Press, 1991.
>   28 p. Illus.
>   A pelican is missing. But inspector Beak solves
>   the case.

> F   Carr, Jon
> Ca   The case of the vanishing canary.
>   Yellow Cage Press, 1993.
>   32 p. Illus.
>   After discovering a diamond the canary vanishes.

Look at both cards. Answer these questions.

1. _____ Who is the author of *The Vanishing Canary?*

2. _____ Who is the author of *The Case of the Missing Pelican?*

3. _____ Which book is illustrated?

4. _____ Which book has more pages?

5. _____ Which book was published first?

6. _____ Which book was published by Pelican Press?

7. _____ Which book is fiction?

8. _____ Which book has a call number F ?
                                                         Ca

9. What is *The Case of the Vanishing Canary* about? _____

_____

10. What is Albert Peterson's story about? _____

_____

NAME _____

COMPARING NONFICTION CATALOG CARDS

---

595   Jamesson, Albert
Ja   Insects in your backyard. Science Press, 1989.
         167 p. Illus.
         Explains what type of insects you can expect to find
         in your backyard.

---

595   Jaterson, Alvin
Ja   Everyday insects. Buggy Press, 1987.
         74 p. Illus.
         Contains pictures of insects and their descriptions.

---

1. _____ Who is the author of *Everyday Insects*?

2. _____ Write the title of the book Albert Jamesson wrote.

3. _____ How many pages are in the book *Everyday Insects*?

4. _____ In what year was *Insects in Your Backyard* made?

5. _____ Is *Everyday Insects* illustrated?

6. _____ In what year was *Everyday Insects* made?

7. _____ Who wrote *Insects in Your Backyard*?

8. _____ Who is the publisher of *Insects in Your Backyard*?

9. _____ How many pages are in *Insects in Your Backyard*?

10. _____ What is *Everyday Insects* about?

COMPARING NONFICTION CATALOG CARDS

567   Birds of America
So   Albert Song. Birds of America.
      Tweet Tweet, New York: Feather Press, 1989.
      167 p. Illus.

597   Insects and Spiders
Mi   Gerry Milker. Insects and Spiders.
      Webb, New York: Stickey Press, 1986.
      185 p. Illus.
      Complete book of insects and spiders.

Read the two catalog cards. Then answer these questions.

1. _____ Who is the author of *Birds of America*?

2. _____ How many pages are in *Insects and Spiders*?

3. _____ Which book has the most pages?

4. _____ Which book is illustrated?

5. _____ Which book is older?

6. _____ Who is the author of *Insects and Spiders*?

7. _____ What is the copyright date of *Birds of America*?

8. _____ Which book was published by Feather Press?

9. _____ What is the call number of *Birds of America*?

10. _____ What is *Insects and Spiders* about?

THE CALL SLIP

Fiction Book Call Slips

Title: _____

Author: _____

Author Letter: _____

Title: _____

Author: _____

Author Letter: _____

Nonfiction Book Call Slips

Title: _____

Author: _____

Author Letter: _____

_____

Title: _____

Author: _____

Author Letter: _____

_____

USING THE DEWEY DECIMAL SYSTEM

You know that fiction is arranged in the library in alphabetical order. Nonfiction is arranged in number order. Each nonfiction book belongs in one of ten subject divisions, and each division is divided into other classifications. This system is called the Dewey Decimal System. It was created by Melvil Dewey and is used in libraries throughout the United States.

Let's look at the divisions:

000–099   *General Works* has reference books such as encyclopedias, magazines, and newspapers.

100–199   *Philosophy* has books about the ideas of humankind.

200–299   *Religion* has books about different religions, such as Christianity, Judaism, Hinduism, or any other religion.

300–399   *Social Sciences* has books that deal with people and how their society works. That is, books about government, laws, customs of a people, and even the stories of a country. Fables, folk tales, and fairy tales are included in this division.

400–499   The *Language* division has books that teach you about English, as well as other languages such as French, German, or Spanish.

500–599   *Science* contains books about rocks, animals, space, mathematics, etc.

600–699   *Technology (Applied Sciences)* contains books about the human-made arts. For example, books about how to make roads would be in this division. Also, books about transportation, cooking, and farming.

700–799   *Fine Arts* has books that give information about painting, drawing, art, music, and sports.

800–899   The *Literature* division will have books of plays, poems, short stories, and novels.

900–999   The *History and Geography* division will have books about history, travel, geography, and biography. You will also find atlases in this section.

You will be able to browse more effectively if you know what is in each Dewey division.

Dewey Decimal Classification—
The 100 Divisions

000	**Generalities**	**500**	**Pure Sciences**
010	Bibliography	510	Mathematics
020	Library & information sciences	520	Astronomy & allied sciences
030	General encyclopedic works	530	Physics
040		540	Chemistry & allied sciences
050	General serial publications	550	Sciences of earth & other worlds
060	General organizations & museology	560	Paleontology Paleozoology
070	Journalism, publishing, newspapers	570	Life sciences
080	General collections	580	Botanical sciences
090	Manuscripts & book rarities	590	Zoological sciences
100	**Philosophy**	**600**	**Technology (Applied Sciences)**
110	Metaphysics	610	Medical sciences Medicine
120	Epistemology, causation, humankind	620	Engineering & allied operations
130	Paranormal phenomena & arts	630	Agriculture & related technologies
140	Specific philosophical viewpoints	640	Home economics & family living
150	Psychology	650	Management & auxiliary services
160	Logic	660	Chemical & related technologies
170	Ethics (Moral philosophy)	670	Manufacturers
180	Ancient, medieval, Oriental	680	Manufacture for specific uses
190	Modern Western philosophy	690	Buildings
200	**Religion**	**700**	**The Arts**
210	Natural religion	710	Civic & landscape art
220	Bible	720	Architecture
230	Christian theology	730	Plastic arts Sculpture
240	Christian moral & devotional	740	Drawing, decorative & minor arts
250	Local church & religious orders	750	Painting & paintings
260	Social & ecclesiastical theology	760	Graphic arts Prints
270	History & geography of church	770	Photography & photographs
280	Christian denominations & sects	780	Music
290	Other & comparative religious	790	Recreational & performing arts
300	**Social Sciences**	**800**	**Literature**
310	Statistics	810	American literature in English
320	Political science	820	English & Anglo-Saxon literatures
330	Economics	830	Literatures of Germanic languages
340	Law	840	Literatures of Romance languages
350	Public administration	850	Italian, Romanian, Rhaeto-Romanic
360	Social problems & services	860	Spanish & Portuguese literatures
370	Education	870	Italic literatures Latin
380	Commerce (Trade)	880	Hellenic literatures Greek
390	Customs, etiquette, folklore	890	Literatures of other languages
400	**Language**	**900**	**Geography and History**
410	Linguistics	910	General geography Travel
420	English & Anglo-Saxon languages	920	General biography & genealogy
430	Germanic languages German	930	General history of ancient world
440	Romance languages French	940	General history of Europe
450	Italian, Romanian, Rhaeto-Romanic	950	General history of Asia
460	Spanish & Portuguese languages	960	General history of Africa
470	Italic languages Latin	970	General history of North America
480	Hellenic Classical Greek	980	General history of South America
490	Other languages	990	General history of other areas

Reproduced from Edition 11 of the Dewey Decimal Classification, published in 1979, by permission of the Forest Press Division, Lake Placid Education Foundation, owner of copyright.

MY OWN DEWEY DECIMAL CHART

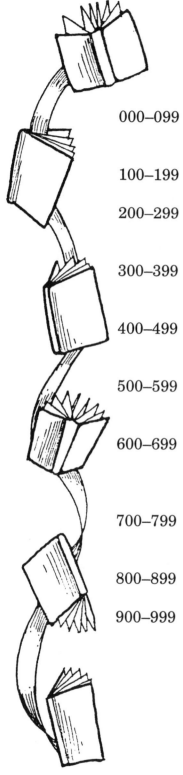

000–099	*General Works*	Encyclopedias, magazines, newspapers
100–199	*Philosophy*	Human ideas
200–299	*Religion*	The Bible, denominations, world religions
300–399	*Social Sciences*	Laws, governments, fairy tales, folktales, customs
400–499	*Language*	Dictionaries, grammar, French, German, Spanish, etc.
500–599	*Science*	Rocks, animals, insects, mathematics, solar system
600–699	*Technology (Applied Sciences)*	(how things work) cooking, pet care, how roads are made, farming
700–799	*Fine Arts*	painting, photography, arts and crafts, sports, music
800–899	*Literature*	poems, plays, short stories
900–999	*History and Geography*	history, travel, geography, biography, atlases

WHAT DEWEY DIVISIONS?

Review the Dewey System, and then write the subject division under which you would find the following: (Use a Dewey Decimal System Chart to help you.)

1. rocks	_____	16. Civil War	_____
2. Bibles	_____	17. geography	_____
3. tennis	_____	18. travel	_____
4. sculpture	_____	19. plays	_____
5. logic	_____	20. short stories	_____
6. birds	_____	21. stars	_____
7. fairy tales	_____	22. music	_____
8. toads	_____	23. poems	_____
9. German	_____	24. Spanish	_____
10. rocks	_____	25. hockey	_____
11. pet care	_____	26. laws	_____
12. Catholicism	_____	27. atlas	_____
13. fish	_____	28. planets	_____
14. paintings	_____	29. cooking	_____
15. baseball	_____	30. encyclopedia	_____

PUTTING BOOK TITLES
IN DEWEY CATEGORIES

Learn how to use the Dewey System by writing in the numerical division and category after each title. Let's say you need a book about ants. In what section will you find all the books about ants? In the 500–599 science section.

Example: *Ants and Their Homes*—500–599 Science

Write the correct Dewey section and number for each book title.

1. *Bees and Wasps*   _____

2. *What's the Weather?*   _____

3. *Stories to Laugh At*   _____

4. *Hobbies for Kids*   _____

5. *Cooking for Kids*   _____

6. *Butterflies*   _____

7. *Mars*   _____

8. *Band Instruments*   _____

9. *Bicycles*   _____

10. *Football Basics*   _____

11. *Arts and Crafts for Kids*   _____

12. *The American Encyclopedia*   _____

13. *Chinese for Beginners*   _____

14. *Poems for Kids*   _____

15. *The History of Africa*   _____

16. *Spanish Sayings*   _____

17. *Travel through Australia*   _____

18. *Learning How to Fly Kites*   _____

19. *Pet Care: The Guinea Pig*   _____

20. *Franklin D. Roosevelt—A Biography* _____

NAME _____

PUTTING BOOK TITLES
IN DEWEY CATEGORIES

Learn how to use the Dewey System by writing in the numerical division and category after each title. Let's say you need a book about ocean shells. In what section will you find all the books about shells? In the 500–599 science section.

Example: *Shells and Coral*—500–599 Science

Write the correct Dewey section and number for each book title.

1. *Dinosaurs and Other Ancient Animals* _____

2. *Famous Explorers* _____

3. *Learning French* _____

4. *Skateboarding* _____

5. *Pet Care: Cats and Kittens* _____

6. *The History of India* _____

7. *Easy Science Experiments* _____

8. *Rocks and Minerals* _____

9. *Religions of the World* _____

10. *Cowboys of the Wild West* _____

11. *Fun Plays for Children* _____

12. *Zebras in the Wild* _____

13. *My First Bible* _____

14. *Short Stories for Young People* _____

15. *Lions and the Wild Country* _____

16. *Fairy Tales of the World* _____

17. *Snails* _____

18. *Japanese Culture and Tradition* _____

19. *Baking for Kids* _____

20. *The Student's Atlas* _____

NAME _____

PUTTING BOOK TITLES
IN DEWEY CATEGORIES

Read the Dewey Decimal System chart and the book titles.
Write the correct Dewey section.

1. *Bees and Wasps* _____

2. *What's the Weather?* _____

3. *Stories to Laugh At* _____

4. *Hobbies for Kids* _____

5. *Cooking for Kids* _____

6. *Butterflies* _____

7. *Mars* _____

8. *Band Instruments* _____

9. *Bicycles* _____

10. *Football Basics* _____

11. *Arts and Crafts for Kids* _____

12. *The American Encyclopedia* _____

13. *Chinese for Beginners* _____

14. *Poems for Kids* _____

15. *The History of Africa* _____

16. *Spanish Sayings* _____

17. *Travel through Australia* _____

18. *Learning How to Fly Kites* _____

19. *Pet Care: The Guinea Pig* _____

20. *Franklin D. Roosevelt—A Biography* _____

PUTTING BOOK TITLES
IN DEWEY CATEGORIES

Read the Dewey Decimal System chart and the book titles.
Write the correct Dewey section.

1. *The Life of Jim Henson: Muppets & Puppets* _____

2. *Trees of North America* _____

3. *Stars, Galaxies, and Space* _____

4. *Cars, Boats, and Trucks* _____

5. *Starfish and other Sea Animals* _____

6. *The Presidents and their Lives* _____

7. *Stange Birds and other Wonders of Science* _____

8. *The Geography of the United States* _____

9. *The Life of Michael Jordan* _____

10. *The Planets* _____

11. *Learning Spanish* _____

12. *Baseball: Rules of the Game* _____

13. *Treating Your Pet Well* _____

14. *Space and Science* _____

15. *Kitten Care* _____

16. *Ice Hockey for Beginners* _____

17. *Learning About the Solar System* _____

18. *Learning about Machines* _____

19. *Gerbils as Pets* _____

20. *Soccer!* _____

PUTTING BOOK TITLES
IN DEWEY CATEGORIES

Read the Dewey Decimal System chart and the book titles.
Write the correct Dewey section.

1. *Cooking for Kids* _____

2. *The Geography of Spain* _____

3. *Learning French* _____

4. *Rabbit Pet Care Manual* _____

5. *Spiders and Other Insects* _____

6. *Magic for Kids* _____

7. *Plays for Beginners* _____

8. *Arts and Crafts for Everyone* _____

9. *Poems for Everyday* _____

10. *Baseball for Juniors* _____

11. *Neptune: An Exciting Planet* _____

12. *The Space Shuttle* _____

13. *The Biography of James Marshall* _____

14. *Hockey: A Great Game* _____

15. *Birds of Prey* _____

16. *The Life of Thomas Jefferson* _____

17. *Whales* _____

18. *History of the Wild West* _____

19. *Manatees: The Sea Cow* _____

20. *The Tall Tale of Pecos Bill* _____

THE DEWEY LADDER

On the following two pages you can record the books you've read using the rungs on the Dewey ladder.

MY FAVORITE STORIES

_____

_____

FAIRY TALES

_____

_____

POETRY

_____

_____

BIOGRAPHIES

_____

_____

ADVENTURE

_____

_____

HISTORY

_____

_____

SCIENCE

_____

_____

PLAYS

_____

_____

USING THE
TABLE OF CONTENTS:
THE MAGAZINE

A table of contents works as a guide for you. In a magazine, the table of contents will give you much information. You can find the title of the story, the author's name and the page number of the story. And, you can get all this information just from the table of contents page.

A table of contents can save you time and work. If you need to know what is in the magazine, skim the table of contents. You need not read or glance through the entire magazine. Use the table of contents instead.

You will find the table of contents at the beginning of the magazine. The stories or articles are listed in the order they appear in the magazine. If you need information about the magazine itself, check this page. Or check the following page. Here you will find how much the magazine costs and its mailing address.

The table of contents can be very helpful. Use it.

USING MAGAZINE TABLE OF CONTENTS

The table of contents can give you much information for your research and reports. Read this table of contents. Then answer the questions.

COOKING MAGAZINE

Learning to Cook: A guide for Kids 34
    by James Stove
Baking Cookies 38
    by Cookie Crumb
Buying the Right Ingredients 49
    by James Checklist
Using Flour in Your Recipes 51
    by Wendy Wheat
Baking Special Holiday Treats 17
    by Holly J. Holiday
Baking Cakes 27
    by Mark Marble
Nutrition and Baking 21
    by Vera Vitamins
How to Cook Vegetables 23
    by Barbara Broccoli
Buying a Cook Book.. 13
    by the editors of *Cooking Up a Storm*

---

1. _____ What article will give you information about nutrition and baking?

2. _____ What article will guide you in cooking?

3. _____ What article will give you information about cakes?

4. _____ Is there any information about vitamins and cooking?

5. _____ What article will help you collect recipes?

6. _____ What article will give you information about holiday cooking?

7. _____ What article will give you information about buying a cookbook?

8. _____ What article was written with young people in mind?

9. _____ What article will help you bake cookies?

10. _____ What article will have a recipe for corn on the cob?

USING MAGAZINE TABLE OF CONTENTS

The table of contents can give you much information for your research and reports. Read this table of contents. Then answer the questions.

1. _____ What article will help you learn about swimming safety rules?

2. _____ What article will tell you about karate?

3. _____ Where will you find information about baseball?

4. _____ What article will give you information about skateboarding rules?

5. _____ What article did Charles Chop write?

6. _____ What article did Bobby Base write?

7. _____ Where can you find information about sports for kids?

8. _____ Where can you learn more about rollerblading?

9. _____ What article did Steven Shotzu write?

10. _____ What article will you find on page 47?

USING MAGAZINE TABLE OF CONTENTS

The table of contents can give you much information for your research and reports. Read this table of contents. Then answer the questions.

How to Build Paper Toys	13
by Patty Paper	
Dollhouses and Building Doll Furniture	15
by Hattie House	
Making Kites	19
by Helen Hightale	
Collecting Baseball Cards	21
by Calvin Card	
Collecting Records	23
by Peter Song	
Making Paintings and Other Crafts	24
by Bart Brushstroke	
Collecting Things: A Children's Guide	27
by Louie Collector	
Hobbies for Kids..	34
by John Fun	
Hobbies Kids Love	51
by R.R. Hobbymaster	
Learning to Collect: A Kid's Guide	57
by Connie Collect	

1. _____ You want to learn about hobbies. What two articles will help?

   _____

2. _____ How to collect baseball cards. What article will help?

3. _____ How do you make a good kite? What article will help?

4. _____ Are there any rules for collecting things? What two articles will help?

   _____

5. _____ How do you collect records? Name the article.

6. _____ Your dollhouse needs work. Name the article.

7. _____ What article did R.R. Hobbymaster write?

8. _____ How do you paint? What article will help?

9. _____ Where can you learn about arts and crafts? What article will help?

USING A MAGAZINE GUIDE

A magazine index guide is a magazine that lists magazines. It lists the stories you can find in these magazines. And it lists the information alphabetically. Usually the information is listed by the subject. For example, let's say you need a story about dinosaurs. How many magazines have articles about dinosaurs? How would you find this information? You would check under "dinosaurs." And finding all the titles of magazines that have stories about dinosaurs would save you time and work.

Each magazine listing is called an *entry*. Lets look at a typical entry for dinosaurs.

---

(1) DINOSAURS: (2) see also ancient reptiles
                  (3) Dinosaurs of Long Ago   (4) Robert Stone
                  (5) Dinosaur Magazine   (6) October 1989.
                  (7) p. 3–10.

Now let's look at each part.

1. This gives you the subject—Dinosaurs.

2. This gives you other subjects you may check for information—See also ancient reptiles.

3. This gives you the title of the magazine article—"Dinosaurs of Long Ago."

4. This gives you the author's name—Robert Stone.

5. This gives you the magazine that has the article—Dinosaur Magazine.

6. This gives you the month, week, and the year that the magazine was published—October 11, 1989.

7. This gives you the page number of the magazine article—pages 3–10.

Let's look at an example:
On what pages will you find the article called "Dinosaurs of Long Ago?"
Answer: pages 3–10.

MAGAZINE INDEX

Hobbies

    All Around Hobbies for Rainy Days. Robert Stone. Hobby Digest Magazine. September 1989. p. 17–23.

    Better Hobbies for Ten Year Olds. Peter Breck. Hobby Magazine. October 1989. p. 3–9.

    Collecting Coins. Alice Coiner. Coin Magazine. December 1987. p. 51–59.

    Collecting Dolls. James Dollar. January 1988. p. 31–36.

    Drawing for Kids. Arthur Brush. Art and Craft Magazine. February 1986. p. 36–39.

    Painting for Young People. Jay Brush. Art and Craft Magazine. March 1987. p. 39–43.

    Records and Music for Young People. James Note. Music Magazine. May 1989. p. 71–79.

1. _____ On what pages will you find "Painting for Young People?"

2. _____ "Records and Music for Young People" is in what magazine?

3. _____ "Drawing for Kids" is in what magazine?

4. _____ "Collecting Coins" is in what magazine?

5. _____ On what pages will you find "Better Hobbies for Ten Year Olds?"

6. _____ "All Around Hobbies for Rainy Days" is in what magazine?

7. _____ "Collecting Dolls" begins on what page?

8. _____ "Painting for Young People" is in what magazine?

9. _____ "Records and Music for Young People" begins on what page?

10. _____ "All Around Hobbies for Rainy Days" begins on what page?

MAGAZINE INDEX

Sports

Baseball Tips for Kids. Rita Base. Sport Magazine. September 1989. p. 3–7.

Basketball Stars and Legends. John Court. Junior Sport Magazine. October 1989. p. 13–19.

Choosing a Sport. James Court. Hobby Magazine. November 1988. p. 27–31.

Football's Famous Players. Roger Runner. Sport Magazine. December 1989. p. 21–25.

Ice Skating Rules for Safety. Susan Ice. Junior Sport Magazine. February 1989. p. 51–55.

Judo and Karate for Young People. Ray Chop. Sport Magazine. March 1987. p. 31–39.

Kites: How to Make Them and How to Fly Them. Richard String. Sport Magazine. April 1989. p. 61–68.

1. _____ "Kites: How to Make Them and How to Fly Them" is on what page?

2. _____ "Judo and Karate for Young People" is in what magazine?

3. _____ On what page will you find" Ice Skating Rules for Safety?"

4. _____ "Choosing a Sport" is in what magazine?

5. _____ On what pages will you find "Basketball Stars and Legends?"

6. _____ In what magazine will you find "Baseball Tips for Kids?"

7. _____ On what page will you find "Baseball Tips for Kids?"

8. _____ "Football's Famous Players" is in what magazine?

9. _____ On what pages will you find "Football's Famous Players?"

10. _____ "Choosing a Sport" is on what pages?

NAME _____

MAGAZINE INDEX

Ancient Animals. Robert Dino. Magazine of Great Dinosaurs. Sept. 1988. p. 7–10.

Can We Ever Know Why the Dinosaur Disappeared? T. Book. Dinosaur Magazine. Oct. 1989. p. 3–12.

Did the Dinosaur Eat Plants? Peter Stone. Science Magazine. November 1989. p. 13–18.

Great Dinosaurs. John Fossil. Science World Magazine. December 1989. p. 40–49.

Ice Age and Dinosaurs. Arthur Fostone. History and Science Magazine. January 1989. p. 3–16.

Land, Fossils, and Dinosaurs. James Speck. Science Magazine, February 1989. p. 10–20.

Small Dinosaurs. Sally Dinston. Science Magazine. March 1989. p. 31–37.

1. _____ What magazine has the story "Small Dinosaurs?"

2. _____ "Did the Dinosaur Eat Plants?" is on what page?

3. _____ What magazine has the story "Did the Dinosaur Eat Plants?"

4. _____ What magazine has the story "Land, Fossils, and the Dinosaurs?"

5. _____ "Ice Age and Dinosaurs" is in what magazine?

6. _____ "Great Dinosaurs" is in what magazine?

7. _____ "Can We Ever Know Why the Dinosaur Disappeared?" is on what page?

8. _____ "Ancient Animals" is in what magazine?

9. _____ "Small Dinosaurs" is on what pages?

10. _____ "Great Dinosaurs" is on what pages?

USING MAGAZINES FOR RESEARCH

There will be times when you will need information from magazines. There are many different types of magazines. It is a good idea to get to know what magazines your library owns. And, it is helpful to know what subjects you can find in these magazines. Sometimes you can tell what subjects you will find in these magazines by reading their titles. You can browse in these magazines by reading their titles. You can browse through the table of contents to get more information.

Magazines can offer you much information. The information you will find in magazines is up-to-date. Sometimes you will be able to find the most recent information on a subject in a magazine. Magazines can offer this type of information because they appear so often. Magazines usually appear monthly. But, remember magazines can also appear every other month.

Now let's look at magazine titles and get a better understanding what they can offer you.

USING MAGAZINES IN YOUR RESEARCH

Singing Monthly Magazine　　*Dancing Magazine*
Drawing for Kids　　　　　　*Karate for Kids*
Skateboarding Magazine　　　*Hockey Digest*
Baseball Digest　　　　　　 *Famous Sports People Magazine*
Football Digest　　　　　　 *Painting Monthly*

What magazine will help in each question?

1. _____ What magazine will help you learn about painting?

2. _____ You sing well. What magazine might you enjoy?

3. _____ You think football is great. What magazine will give you more information?

4. _____ You want information about famous people in sports. What magazine will help?

5. _____ Kick! Chop! Kick! What magazine will help give you more information?

6. _____ You plan to learn about painting. What magazine will give you more information?

7. _____ You plan to draw your next cover for your report. What magazine will help?

8. _____ You are interested in dancing. What magazine will help?

9. _____ Baseball. You want to read more about it. What magazine will help?

10. _____ What are the rules for street hockey? You want to find more information about hockey. What magazine will help?

NAME _____

USING MAGAZINES

Which magazine would help you in each research situation?

Shark and Sea Life Magazine   *Dog and Cat Magazine*
Whales   *Animals of the Wild*
Science Magazine for Kids   *Sports for Kids*
American History For Kids   *Poem and Play Magazine*
Weather Magazine   *Insect Digest*

1. _____ You are writing a report about clouds. What magazine might help?

2. _____ You are writing a report about sharks. What magazine might help?

3. _____ You need information about the cowboys in the Wild West. What magazine might help?

4. _____ You need a picture of the wild animal, the tiger. What magazine might help?

5. _____ Your class will put on a play next month. Where can you find a good play?

6. _____ You need a picture of a purple grasshopper. What magazine will help?

7. _____ You need some help. Where can you find a science experiment for your science class?

8. _____ You plan to draw a poster of common cats for your animal report. What magazine might help?

9. _____ You need a poem for Ground Hog Day. What magazine has poems?

10. _____ You need a picture of whales. What magazine will help?

NAME _____

USING MAGAZINES

Which magazine would help you in each research situation?

Cooking For Kids   President Magazine
Dinosaur Magazine   Famous Biographies Magazine
American History for Kids   Painting for Kids
Wild West Magazine   States Magazine
Early Explorers Magazine   Music Magazine for Kids

1. _____ You plan a report about cowboys and the Wild West. What magazine might help you?

2. _____ You plan a report about Christopher Columbus. What magazine might help you?

3. _____ Where can you learn about the American colonies?

4. _____ What is the latest in music? What magazine might help you?

5. _____ You are writing a report about New Jersey. What magazine might help you?

6. _____ You are planning a report about Walt Disney. What magazine might help you?

7. _____ Your class will visit a museum. Your group will see the dinosaur exhibit. What magazine might give you more information?

8. _____ Your teacher assigned you a report about George Washington the first President. What magazine might help you?

9. _____ What magazine will help you learn about cooking?

10. _____ What is the latest song and dance? What magazine will help you?

NAME _____

USING MAGAZINES

Which magazine would help you in each research situation?

Weather Experiments for Kids   *Nutrition Magazine*
Science Experiments for Kids   *Fashion Style Magazine*
Sports for Kids   *Learning About Animals*
Collecting Rocks and Shells   *Learning About Chemicals*
Plant and Garden Magazine   *Your Environment*

1. _____ You are writing a report about clouds. What magazine might help?

2. _____ You need information about the latest fashion styles. What magazine will help you?

3. _____ You plan to grow your own garden. What magazine will help you?

4. _____ Are french fries a good food to eat? What magazine might help you answer that question?

5. _____ You enjoy baseball, but you would like to find out about hockey and soccer. What magazine might help you?

6. _____ You plan to show an experiment at the Science Fair. Your subject is magnets. What magazine might help you?

7. _____ You find a strange rock in your backyard. What magazine might help you identify the rock?

8. _____ You found a chipmunk. What magazine might help you learn about this animal?

9. _____ Is it safe to mix chemicals? What magazine might help you?

10. _____ How can you help to protect your environment? What magazine might give you some answers?

USING ENCYCLOPEDIAS

The word "encyclopedia" comes from a Greek word meaning a complete round (circle) or course of learning. Today we use the word **encyclopedia** to mean a set of books in which the various topics from all branches of knowledge are treated in separate articles, usually arranged in alphabetical order.

Encyclopedias are classified in the 000 section of the Dewey Decimal System under "Generalities." However, they are usually kept in a special section of the library which is set aside for reference books.

If you are looking for information about a topic or subject for a report, the encyclopedia is often a good place to start. The article will give you a good general overview of the topic. However, you will usually want to find additional information sources as well. The encyclopedia will give information about persons, places and things, and answer the questions "who?" "where?" "when?" and "how?" But an encyclopedia usually does not answer the question "why?" or discuss both sides of a controversial subject in depth.

In order to become more skillful in using an encyclopedia, there are several things you should learn and remember. They are:

1. How the encyclopedia is arranged.
2. How to use the index or the cross references.
3. How to choose the right keyword when you are looking for a subject.
4. How to use the guide words at the top of each page.
5. How to use the illustrations; including pictures, charts, graphs, maps, diagrams, etc.

Encyclopedias are usually arranged alphabetically. Often you will find that you can turn directly to the volume containing the letter of the alphabet with which your subject begins. For example, if you want an article about "France," you can turn directly to the "F" volume and look for the subject alphabetically. You will also find that such a large subject is divided into parts, perhaps with **subtopics** such as "the climate," "the people," "the industries," etc. The subtopic headings may be labeled in bold-faced type.

CHOOSING THE CORRECT ENCYCLOPEDIA VOLUME

A	B	C-Ch	Ci-Cz	D	E	F	G	H	I	J-K	L	M	N	O-P	Q-R	S	T	U-V	W-X-Y-Z
1	2	3	4	5	6	7	8	9	10	11	12	13	14	15	16	17	18	19	20

Above is an illustration of the volumes of a set of encyclopedias. In which volume would you find information on each of the following subjects? Write only the volume number on the blank.

_____ 1. Dolphins   _____ 11. Washington, D.C.

_____ 2. Pheasants   _____ 12. Computers

_____ 3. Massachusetts   _____ 13. Wheat

_____ 4. Rubber   _____ 14. Koala

_____ 5. Ships   _____ 15. Paper

_____ 6. Toys   _____ 16. Dolls

_____ 7. Egypt   _____ 17. Ice Age

_____ 8. Anatomy   _____ 18. Diamonds

_____ 9. Libraries   _____ 19. X-rays

_____ 10. Winds   _____ 20. Thomas Jefferson

KEYWORDS

When a topic has more than one word, it may be difficult to choose the correct keyword to look for in the encyclopedia. Here are a few general rules:

1. You will find information about a person under his or her last name.
   George Washington would be found under "W" for Washington.

2. If a person has a title, you will find information about him or her under the last part of his/her name.
   Queen Elizabeth would be found under "E" for Elizabeth.
   President Johnson would be found under "J" for Johnson.

3. If a subject has two (or more) parts, you will usually find it under the first part.
   North America would be found under "N" for North.
   Pacific Ocean would be found under "P" for Pacific.
   Space travel would be found under "S" for Space.

4. You will not find words or subjects under their abbreviations. Look for them as if they were spelled out.
   St. Paul (city) would be found under "Sa" for Saint Paul.

5. You will usually find a subject under the more specific topic name. For example, look for Baseball under "B" for Baseball, not "S" for Sports. However, if you are not sure which word to look under, the index or cross references will help you. Also note the additional topics listed under the main topics in the index or the cross references, also.

ENCYCLOPEDIA KEYWORDS

Circle the word which you think will lead you to the most information about the following topics in the encyclopedia. Then write the letter of the volume of the encyclopedia in the blank.

A	B	C-Ch	Ci-Cz	D	E	F	G	H	I	J-K	L	M	N	O-P	Q-R	S	T	U-V	W-X-Y-Z
1	2	3	4	5	6	7	8	9	10	11	12	13	14	15	16	17	18	19	20

1. _____ The use of atomic energy

2. _____ The history of the Republican Party

3. _____ The birthplace of President Franklin D. Roosevelt

4. _____ The members of the North Atlantic Treaty Organization

5. _____ The population of New Zealand

6. _____ The location of the Indian Ocean

7. _____ The population of St. Louis, Missouri

8. _____ The birthday of Queen Elizabeth II of Great Britain

9. _____ The nationality of Sir Isaac Newton

10. _____ The uses of guided missiles

11. _____ The location of Rocky Mountain National Park

12. _____ The rules for playing ice hockey

13. _____ The history of motion pictures

14. _____ The number of post offices in the United States

15. _____ President U.S. Grant's middle name

16. _____ The location of Prince Edward Island

17. _____ The author of the book *The Hunchback of Notre Dame*

18. _____ The cause of typhoid fever

19. _____ The name of the President of Mexico

20. _____ The difference between a meteor and a meteorite

USING ENCYCLOPEDIA CROSS-REFERENCES

If you need more information for your report, look at the very end of the encyclopedia article. Here you will find other places to search for information. These places are called *cross-references.* They are the topics under which you can find related information about your topic. Let's say you found information about the postal service under postal service. Now look at the cross-reference.

Postal Service – see also airmail:
                              pony express; stamps

The *see also references* show you where to look or see also additional information. These references are written in alphabetical order so they are easy to use. Remember *see also references* are another source for you to check. If you find additional information in a second encyclopedia article, check the end of this article too. It may give another article to check. Most articles have see also references. This is a valuable tool. It may make the search easier and a lot more fun!

Check the see also references for the article on the postal service. You will find articles on each of the following:

AIRMAIL
PONY EXPRESS
STAMPS

SEE ALSO REFERENCES

Look at this see also reference. Write the see also reference that will help you find information for each question.

> Transportation — see also airplanes;
> automobiles; highways; railroads;
> ships; and travel

1. vacation travel _____

2. early sailing vessels _____

3. the Wright brothers first plane _____

4. the model T car _____

5. mail planes _____

6. traveling across the country _____

7. learning to fly _____

8. the differences between boats and ships _____

9. racing cars _____

10. antique cars _____

THE DICTIONARY

The dictionary is a book that contains a lists of words in alphabetical order. You can use the dictionary to look up how a word is spelled, what the word means, and how the word is pronounced.

In addition to learning the;

- **Spelling** of the word,
- the **meaning** of the word, and
- how the word is **pronounced**,

you can also use the dictionary for:

- **Illustrations** – Often the dictionary uses illustrations to help clarify the meaning of the word.

- **Parts of Speech** – The dictionary uses symbols to show the grammatical use of the word. The common are: *(adj.)* for *adjective, (n.)* for *noun,* and *(v.t. or v.i.)* or *verb.*

- **Phrases/Sentences** – The word that you have looked up will also be used in a sentences to help you understand its meanings.

- **Synonym** – The dictionary often provides synonyms (words which have nearly the same meaning). Synonym words follow the definition of the word.

THESAURUS

A thesaurus is a book of synonyms. Synonyms are words that have almost the same meaning, like "happy" and "cheerful." A thesaurus can give you new choices for words instead of using the same words over and over again. A thesaurus can also help you pick exactly the word you want to write.

THE DICTIONARY

Compound words are often written incorrectly, not because they are spelled wrong, but because a word may need a hypen, a space between the two words, or else because a word needs to be written with no space or hypens. If you are unsure about these types of words – the dictionary is the place to go!

Read the words below. Are they written correctly? If so, write the word "correct." If not, write them correctly, using the dictionary for help.

1. grandfather   _____

2. one half   _____

3. bird-watching   _____

4. great grandfather   _____

5. checkbook   _____

6. head ache   _____

7. green house   _____

8. textbook   _____

9. vice president   _____

10. mother in law   _____

11. stomach ache   _____

12. world wide   _____

13. mini bike   _____

14. half-hearted   _____

NAME _____

THE DICTIONARY

Did you know that there are many words in a dictionary that have more than one meaning? Some words might have seven or eight! Read the words below, then look them up in the dictionary and write (in your own words) three different meanings for each word.

1. down: _____

_____

_____

2. tip: _____

_____

_____

3. last: _____

_____

_____

4. bend: _____

_____

_____

5. slip: _____

_____

_____

6. part: _____

_____

_____

7. pound: _____

_____

_____

8. fly: _____

_____

_____

9. title: _____

_____

_____

10. note: _____

_____

_____

NAME _____

THE THESAURUS

A thesaurus is a book of synonyms. Synonyms are words that have almost the same meaning, like "happy" and "cheerful." A thesaurus can give you new choices for words instead of using the same words over and over again. A thesaurus can also help you pick exactly the word you want to write. Look at each of the following words, then use a thesaurus to write two synonyms of each word.

1. smart   _____   _____

2. neat   _____   _____

3. job   _____   _____

4. empty   _____   _____

5. frown   _____   _____

6. crowd   _____   _____

7. help   _____   _____

8. brave   _____   _____

9. ill   _____   _____

10. almost   _____   _____

THE THESAURUS

Read the following story. Fill in the blanks with synonyms of the circled words in parentheses. Use a thesaurus if you need help. The first one has been done for you.

THE BEAR AND THE BEES

Once there was a (big) __**large**__ brown bear who lived inside a cave with his wife.

"Please, dear," she said to him one day, " (run) _____ down to the brook and catch some fish for dinner. But don't go near the beehive in the old dead tree. Remember what the bees did to you last time!"

The big brown bear (walked) _____ slowly toward the brook. Before he knew it, he was at the old tree.

As soon as he reached the tree, he (pushed) _____ his paw into the hive and grabbed a piece of honeycomb. Inside the busy bees were making wax and honey.

But the minute they saw that (big) _____ paw (wrecking) _____ their home and stealing their precious honey, they rushed out!

Swarming after him in a big cloud, the bees were ready to (zoom) _____ down on his head. So the poor bear had to act (fast) _____. Pulling and kicking and tugging, he tore himself loose at last, leaving a great deal of his fur in the brush. He ran toward the brook, jumped into the water, and hid there with only his nose showing. Suddenly the bees spotted him and swooped down smack on his nose.

"Ouch! Ouch!" he cried and ran out of the brook into a grassy field. And he was supposed to (catch) _____ some fish for dinner!

Back he went to the brook and quickly caught up with a trout. Then he ran toward home, looking over his shoulder fearfully.

He was so (happy) _____ to be home that he gave his wife a great big bear hug and kissed her on both ears. His wife was quite (surprised) _____ by such a greeting and guessed right away he had done something (wrong) _____. And as soon as she saw his nose, she knew what he had done.

She (asked) _____ him why he went near those bees but he gave no (excuse) _____. He promised his wife he would never go near that tree again. She gave him the (biggest) _____ piece of trout and bandaged his nose. But deep down inside he wished the trout would have been some of that nice honey.

PARTS OF A BOOK

Although there are millions and millions of books, and each one is different in shape, color, size, topic and length, all books have the same format – or the way in which they are put together.

ON THE OUTSIDE

All books have a **cover**. The cover tells the very basic information about the book. On the cover you will find the **title**, (the name of the book) and the author's name. If the book has pictures you might also find the illustrator's name.

The **spine** of the book is the thin side of a book that holds the pages together. On the spine you will see the title; the author's name; the publisher; and if the book is in the library, you might even find the call number on the spine. Information is put on the spine so that if you are looking for books on a shelf, they will be very easy to find.

(Note: Some paperback books are very thin, so they do not always have a spine. These books are either stapled or saddle-stitched.)

THE TITLE PAGE

The **title page** is found at the beginning of a book. On this page you will see the full title of the book; the author's name and if there are pictures, the illustrator's name. (If a book has pictures and only the author's name appears on the title page, you can assume that the author is also the illustrator.)

On the title page you will also find the **publisher's** name. This is the company where the book was put together and made ready for sale. After the publisher's name you will see the **place of publication** – the city in which the book was made. Sometimes a book may be printed in more than one city, then all of the cities will be listed.

On the other side of the title page (verso), you will find the date of publication – the **copyright** date. This date will be after the word "copyright," or after the symbol for copyright which looks like this © (a "c" inside a small circle). On this page you will also find other information that is important to the librarians who put call numbers on the books. For students, however, the copyright date is the most important part of this page.

PARTS OF A BOOK

Title – The name of the book.
Author – The person who wrote the book.
Illustrator – The person who created the pictures.
Publisher – The company that prepared the book for sale.
Place of Publication – The place where the book was made.
Copyright Date – The year that the book was first made.

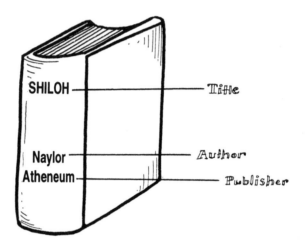

THE TITLE PAGE

Look at the title page in a book of your choice to locate the following information.

Title _____

Author _____

Illustrator _____

Publisher _____

Place of Publication _____

Copyright Date _____

Does your book have a table of contents? _____

Does your book have an index? _____

THE TABLE OF CONTENTS

Many books, especially nonfiction books (books that contain true facts) are divided into several sections to help you quickly locate the information you are looking for. After the title page you will find a listing of these sections on a page (or pages) called the **table of contents**. This part of the book lists all of the chapter names and page numbers that the chapters begin on.

Reading a table of contents will help you find the information you need about a particular subject. Look at the following sample table of contents from a book about earthquakes:

Table of Contents	
Cracks and faults	page 4
Continental drifting	page 6
Earthquakes in the ocean	page 9
Measuring earthquakes	page 11
Most damaging earthquakes in history	page 14
Earthquake prediction	page 16
Protection from earthquakes	page 19
Preventing earthquakes	page 21

Now write the page number of the chapter that would most likely answer the questions: Where would you find information on;

1. the earthquake that caused the most damage? _____

2. instruments used to signal an earthquake is on the way? _____

3. where the continents have split and moved apart? _____

4. what builders have done to keep tall buildings safe? _____

5. how pumping water into the earth can stop earthquakes? _____

6. the San Francisco earthquake of 1906? _____

7. "clues" that tell scientists when an earthquake is coming? _____

8. the difference between cracks and faults? _____

9. the scale used to tell how bad an earthquake is? _____

USING A BOOK INDEX

Like a table of contents, an ***index*** is also commonly found in nonfiction books. Unlike a table of contents, which is in the front of a book and lists the general topics in the order they appear in the book, the index is found in the very back of the book and lists specific topics and keywords alphabetically. For instance, if you were doing a report on Hawaii and you had a book called The Fifty States, you could look in the index under "H" to find the "Hawaii" entry. All page numbers would be listed on which the word "Hawaii" appears in the book.

Main headings in the index often have subheadings to guide you to more specific information. The main headings listed in the sample index below are "Animals," "People," and "Vehicles." The other headings are subheadings.

An index is a list of subjects and keywords found in a book. Many details such as places, names, and definitions are included. How do you use an index? Let's say you choose a book about drawing. Pretend you need to learn how to draw a horse for your report cover. Look at this index from a book on drawing. What is your subject? It is horses. Is there a listing for "Horses?" Yes, on page 32. You can turn to page 32 and find what you need without having to read the whole book about drawing.

NAME _____

USING A BOOK INDEX

You will find the index at the end of the book. It is an alphabetical list of subjects that you can find in the book. If you know how to use an index, you reduce your research time. Look at a sample index below from a book on ants.

ANTS

the body	5
enemies	27
food	13
the nest	7
and people	24
queen	23
types	17
and the weather	24
worker	19

Look at the index above and write the page number where the answers to the following questions can be found.

1. _____ On what pages can you find information about the places where ants might make their nests?

2. _____ Is a drone a type of ant?

3. _____ Are spiders friendly towards ants?

4. _____ Are green plants a good food source for ants?

5. _____ Does an ant have three or five body parts?

6. _____ Is a damp place a good spot for ants to make their nests?

7. _____ Who is the leader of the ant colony?

8. _____ How long do worker ants live?

9. _____ Is there information in this book about the difference between black and brown ants?

10. _____ Can insects be friends of ants?

11. _____ Are nests ever built in dry places?

12. _____ Is there such an ant as the nurse ant?

13. _____ Is there a special way that an ant colony is built?

14. _____ Do termite ants exist?

15. _____ Do ants have antennae?

NAME _____

USING A BOOK INDEX

BUTTERFLIES

caterpillars	6
colors	43
food	17
flowers	31
friends	13
monarch	27
moths	21
sizes	7
types	23
wings	34

Read the book index.
On what page number will you find answers to these questions?

1. _____ Do butterflies ever lose their wings?

2. _____ Are a moth and a butterfly the same insect?

3. _____ What are the sizes of butterflies?

4. _____ How much time does it take for a caterpillar to become a butterfly?

5. _____ Do butterflies really like flowers?

6. _____ What type of food do butterflies eat?

7. _____ Is a spider a friend or enemy of the butterfly?

8. _____ What is the most common color of the butterfly?

9. _____ Is the monarch butterfly really orange or black?

10. _____ How many types of butterflies are there?

11. _____ Is a caterpillar an insect?

12. _____ Do butterflies eat flowers?

13. _____ Is purple the most common color of butterflies?

14. _____ Is pollen a food for butterflies?

15. _____ Is the red-wing a type of butterfly?

NAME _____

USING A BOOK INDEX

BIRDS

Beak	31
Body	3
Claws	17
Colors	64
Feathers	23
Flight	111
Food	39
Nest, location	61
Nest, types	57
Wings	46

Read the index.
On what page number will you find answers to these questions?

1. _____ What page will tell you about what foods birds eat?

2. _____ What page will tell you about the color of birds' feathers?

3. _____ Are all birds' wings the same?

4. _____ Where do birds usually build their nests?

5. _____ Are all nests built of sticks and grasses?

6. _____ Why do birds have different size beaks?

7. _____ How do birds fly?

8. _____ Is purple a common color for birds?

9. _____ Do birds use their claws to catch other birds?

10. _____ Are nests ever built on the ground?

11. _____ Are nests ever built with mud?

12. _____ What kind of bones do birds have?

13. _____ Do birds eat seeds?

14. _____ Do birds fly south?

15. _____ Do birds ever use their beaks to get food?

OVERVIEW—USING A BOOK INDEX

COOKING

baking 3
cookies 13
fried foods 17
household 19
icings 29
pots and pans............................... 21
recipes 41
salty foods 57
vegetables 81
    cooked 91
    raw 97

Read the index.
On what page number will you find answers to these questions?

1. _____ What page will give you information about how to prepare raw vegetables?

2. _____ Where can you find information about baking?

3. _____ On what page will you find a picture of pans?

4. _____ Is there any information about salty foods?

5. _____ Where can you find information about recipes?

6. _____ Is there any information about cooked vegetables?

7. _____ Where can you find information about cookies?

8. _____ Can you find information about fried foods?

9. _____ Is there any information about icing?

10. _____ On what page can you find information about vegetables?

READING A BIBLIOGRAPHY

At the end of a nonfiction book, the author will sometimes include a list of other books that have more information on the same topic they have written about. This is a list of books called a bibliography.

Your teacher, for example may give you a list of books about animals that live in the ocean. If your teacher wanted you to think about writing a report, how would a bibliography help you? Pretend that you are looking for information about sharks. First, lets's look at a sample bibliography:

SEA ANIMALS

Colt, Tara. <u>Whales</u>. New York: Sea Press. 1987.
Darra, James. <u>Sharks</u>. Boston: Howell, 1985.
Goodwin, John. <u>Starfishes</u>. Chicago: Coral Press, 1989.
Holt, Peter. <u>Sharks in the Ocean</u>. New York: Blue Press, 1965.
Jameson, Carlo. <u>Sharks and Their Worlds</u>. Seattle: Ocean Press, 1993.

What three books will help you? The answer is *Sharks, Sharks in the Ocean,* and *Sharks and Their World.* Now look carefully at the information in a bibliography. You can find out the name of the author, book title, publisher, and copyright date. Look for each copyright date for the books about sharks. Which one would give you the most up-to-date information? Answer: *Sharks and Their World.* Which one would give you the oldest information? Answer: *Sharks in the Ocean.*

IMPORTANT NOTE: *The bibliography has a special format that is always used.*
   Author last name, author first name. Title. City: Publisher. Date.

NAME _____

READING A BIBLIOGRAPHY

Read the bibliography. What book would help you answer the questions below?

Antennae, John. Insects in Your Own Backyard. Boston: Wing Press, 1989.

Bugg, Arthur. Insects that Fly. Minneapolis: Spary Press, 1992.

Creeper, Roger. Insects that Crawl. New York: Crawls Press, 1989.

Dug, Martin. Insects that Dig. Seattle: Hole Press. 1987.

Hill, James. Ants. Chicago: Anthill Press, 1990.

Mills, Marta. Strange Facts About Insects. Boston: Science Press, 1979.

Shell, Roger. Beetles. New York: Bugtime Press, 1993.

Shello, Roger. The Insect Encyclopedia. New York: Buggy Time Press, 1989.

Wing, Carla. Butterflies. Chicago: Caterpillar Press, 1993.

1. _____ What book will help you find out about butterflies?

2. _____ Is there such an insect as the Purple Grasshopper?

3. _____ Do caterpillars dig?

4. _____ Do earthworms crawl?

5. _____ How big is an ant hill?

6. _____ Do dragonflies fly?

7. _____ Is the lady bug a beetle?

8. _____ Can you find the praying mantis insect in your backyard?

9. _____ Where can you find information about any insect?

10. _____ Do water bugs really crawl on the surfaces of the water?

USING A BIBLIOGRAPHY

A bibliography can help you get information for your research and reports. Read this bibliography on cooking resources. What books will help you answer the questions?

Cook, Peter. <u>Learning to Cook Dinner Without an Oven</u>. New York: Temperature Press. 1991.

Cooker, James. <u>Kids Guide to Cooking</u>. Stove, NY: Stove Press. 1993.

Flour, Linda. <u>Kids Guide to Cooking for the Holidays</u>. Happytown, NJ: Eaton Press. 1985.

Flour, Peter. <u>Vegetables, Fruits and Kids: What Tastes Good and is Good</u>. Vitamin, NJ: Health Press. 1987.

Flour, Roger. <u>Eating Right Vegetables: Ask Kids</u>. Healthways, NJ: Health Press. 1992.

Pot, James. <u>Baking Cookies: Easy Recipes for Kids</u>. Sweettown, NY: Sugartime Press. 1993.

Pot, Peter. <u>Baking for the Holidays: Help for Kids</u>. Sweettown, NY: Page Press. 1987.

Potts, Richard. <u>Buying a Cookbook for a Young Person</u>. Page, NY: Page Press. 1993.

Stove, James. <u>Collecting Recipes Kids Can Use</u>. Page, NY: Page Press. 1990.

1. _____ What two books were written especially with vegetables in mind?

   _____

2. _____ What two books will help you with holiday cooking?

   _____

3. _____ What book will tell you how to collect recipes?

4. _____ What two books will help you buy a cookbook?

   _____

5. _____ What book will help you bake cookies?

6. _____ What book will help you cook dinner?

7. _____ What book was written by Linda Flour?

NAME _____

OVERVIEW—USING A BIBLIOGRAPHY
Read the bibliography. Answer these questions.

Boxer, Louise. <u>Training Your Dog</u>. Paw Print, NJ: Dogbreath Press. 1987.

Boxton, Roger. <u>Training Your Cat</u>. Meow, NJ: Whisker Press. 1993.

Cat, Susan. <u>A Kids Guide for Choosing a Pet</u>. Pet, NJ: Pet Press. 1990.

Dogger, Roger. <u>Choosing Mice or Gerbils?</u> Pellet, NJ: Cage Press. 1992.

Doggone, June. <u>Setting Up Your Aquarium</u>. Tank, NY: Gravel Press. 1991.

Fish, Arthur. <u>Choosing Fish as Pets</u>. Tank, NY: Bubble Press. 1989.

Gerbil, Louise. <u>Chcosing Hamsters or Guinea Pigs?</u> Scamper, VA: Rodent Press. 1990.

Hank, Sally. <u>Parrots as Pets</u>. Color, NY: Feather Press, 1987.

Kat, Susan. <u>Taking Care of Your Kitten</u>. Purrtown, NY: Meow Press, 1989.

Puppy, Arthur. <u>Taking Care of Your Puppy</u>. Bonetown, NJ: Dogbreath Press. 1987.

1. _____   What two books will help you train your cat?

   _____

2. _____   What three books will help you choose a pet?

   _____

   _____

3. _____   What book will help you set up a fish tank?

4. _____   Is there a book that will give you information about parrots?

5. _____   Is there a book that will help you learn about your hamster?

6. _____   Is there a book that will help you learn about your new gerbil?

7. _____   Can you find information about keeping mice?

8. _____   What two books were published by Dogbreath Press?

   _____

9. _____   What book was written especially for kids?

PARTS OF A BOOK – REVIEW

Place the letter of the word in front of the correct definition.

A. publisher   _____   Outside protection of a book.

B. index   _____   Person who wrote the book.

C. spine   _____   List of chapters in a book.

D. author   _____   Company that prints the book.

E. verso   _____   Name of the book.

F. main heading   _____   Main entries in the index of a book.

G. table of contents   _____   Date the book was published.

H. copyright date   _____   Thin part of a book that holds it together.

I. title   _____   Page in the front of the book that gives the title, author, illustrator, and publisher of the book.

J. cover   _____   List of topics and keywords arranged in alphabetical order in the back of the book with the page number of where the information can be found.

K. place of publication   _____   Secondary entries in the index of the book.

L. title page   _____   The page on the other side of the title page where all of the copyright is found.

M. subheading   _____   City where the book was published.

N. Bibliography   _____   A list of books on a particular subject.

BIOGRAPHY

What is a *biography*? A biography is the true story of someone's life. The call number of a biography is 921. Under this number are the first two letters of the last name of the person who the book is about. What is an *autobiography*? An autobiography is written by the same person that the book is about. The call number works the same as a biography.

What is a *collective biography*? A collective biography is a collection of more than one biography in one book. For example the lives of ten famous baseball players in one book is a collective biography. The call number is 920. Under this number are the first two letters of the last name of the writer of the book.

Examples:

Biography—Life of George Peabody by Tara Bell.

> 921
> Pe

Autobiography—Life of George Peabody by George Peabody.

> 921
> Pe

Collective Biography—The Lives of Famous Scientists by L.C. Hook.

> 920
> Ho

NAME _____

BIOGRAPHIES

Remember:
1. A biography has a call number of 921.
2. A collective biography has a call number of 920.
3. Add the first two letters of the last name of the person the biography is about.
4. A collective biography has the first two letters of the writer's name.

Write call numbers for these **biographies:**

1. _____ *Dolly Madison: Daughter of the American Revolution* by Lynn Ice Cream.

2. _____ *Davy Crockett: Life of a Pioneer* by Ray Counskin.

3. _____ *Mickey Mantle: His Life* by Roy Bat.

4. _____ *Daniel Boone: A Legend* by Roger West.

5. _____ *Betsy Ross: Her Life* by Linda Flagg.

Write call numbers for these **autobiographies:**

1. _____ *Walt Disney: My Story* by Walt Disney.

2. _____ *Mickey Mantle* by Mickey Mantle.

3. _____ *Jim Henson: The Muppets and Me* by Jim Henson.

4. _____ *Daniel Boone: My Life* by Daniel Boone.

5. _____ *Betsy Ross: My Story* by B. Ross.

Write call numbers for these **collective biographies:**

1. _____ *Famous Writers* by Arthur Penn.

2. _____ *Famous Sports Stars* by James Locker.

3. _____ *Famous People and their Stories* by Peter People.

4. _____ *Animals and their Stories* by Roger Cage.

5. _____ *Plays to Enjoy* by Arthur Scene.

BIOGRAPHIES

Remember: 1. A *biography* has a call number of 921.
2. And a *collective biography* has a call number 920.
3. Add the first two letters of the last name of the person the biography is about.
4. But a *collective biography* has the first letters of the *writer's name*.

Write call numbers for these **biographies.**

1. _____ *Captain Hook: A Pirate's Life* by Edward Ho.

2. _____ *Sir Francis Drake: The Explorer* by James Sea.

3. _____ *Betsy Ross: Daughter of the American Revolution* by C.W. Flagg.

4. _____ *The Life of a First Lady: Rosalyn Carter* by P. Carter.

5. _____ *The Life of a President: Jimmy Carter* by J. Carter.

Write call numbers for these **autobiographies**

1. _____ *Dr. Seuss: My Life* by Dr. Seuss.

2. _____ *The Life of a President: Thomas Jefferson* by T. Jefferson.

3. _____ *Babe Ruth: My Story* by Babe Ruth.

4. _____ *Walt Disney: The Life of Walt Disney* by W. Disney.

5. _____ *Mickey Mantle: My Biography* by Mickey Mantle.

Write call numbers for these **collective biographies.**

1. _____ *Famous Rock Stars* by Roger Note.

2. _____ *The Lives of Rock Stars* by Arthur Song.

3. _____ *Famous Cartoonists* by Mel Blank.

4. _____ *Famous Airplane Pilots* by Roger Wing.

5. _____ *Famous Football Players* by Edward Foot.

BIOGRAPHIES

Remember: 1. A *biography* has a call number of 921.
2. And a *collective biography* has a call number 920.
3. Add the first two letters of the last name of the person the biography is about.
4. But a *collective biography* has the first letters of the *writer's name.*

Write call numbers for these **biographies.**

1. _____ *Story of Walt Disney* by Albert Cartoon.

2. _____ *Albert Einstein: His Story* by Robert Math.

3. _____ *Babe Ruth: His Life* by Roger Diamond.

4. _____ *Purple Sage: A Musician's Story* by L.G. Note.

5. _____ *George Washington* by Sally Cherry.

Write call numbers for these **autobiographies.**

1. _____ *Walt Disney: My Life* by Walt Disney.

2. _____ *Albert Einstein: My Life* by Albert Einstein.

3. _____ *Life and Times of Babe Ruth* by Babe Ruth.

4. _____ *Purple Sage: A Songwriter's Life* by P. Sage.

5. _____ *George Washington: My Life* by George Washington.

Write call numbers for these **collective biographies.**

1. _____ *Famous Cartoonists* by John Laugh.

2. _____ *Famous Music Stars* by James Song.

3. _____ *Famous Baseball Players* by Peter Base.

4. _____ *Famous Inventors* by Alvin Experiment.

5. _____ *The Book of Presidents* by W. House

BIOGRAPHIES—COLLECTIVE BIOGRAPHIES

A *collective biography* is a book about more than one person It's call number is 920. The first two letters of the writer's last name follow the number.

Example: *Famous Singers* by Roger Note has a call number of:

920
No

Biographies are books about one person. It's call number is 921. The first two letters of the last name of the person the book is about follow the number.

Example: *All About Walt Disney* by Walter Cartoon has a call number of:

921
Di

Read each title: Write 920 for collective biography.
Write 921 for a single biography.
Add the correct letters to complete the call number.

1. _____ *Story of Christopher Columbus* by Arthur Ship.

2. _____ *Jim Henson: His Story* by James Muppet.

3. _____ *Famous Cartoonists* by Peter Funny.

4. _____ *Famous Explorers* by Roger Map.

5. _____ *Sports Legends* by Roger Bat.

6. _____ *Teddy Roosevelt: A President's Life* by Teddy Power.

7. _____ *The Presidents: Stories and Lives* by James Office.

8. _____ *Babe Ruth: Baseball's Greatest* by James Base.

9. _____ *Story of Dolly Madison* by Edward Furniture.

10. _____ *Baseball Pitchers: Their Stories* by James Glove.

If the book is a biography write "YES." If it is not a biography write "NO."

1. _____ *Rocks and Minerals* by James Stone.

2. _____ *Boats and Trucks* by Peter Wheel.

3. _____ *Dancers: Their Stories* by John Step.

4. _____ *Hamsters* by Alice Cage.

BIOGRAPHIES—COLLECTIVE BIOGRAPHIES

A *collective biography* is a book about more than one person It's call number is 920. The first two letters of the writer's last name follow the number.

Example: *All About Sports Stars* by Roger Base has a call number of:

920
Ba

Biographies are books about one person. It's call number is 921. The first two letters of the last name of the person the book is about follow the number.

Example: *All About Babe Ruth* by Roger Base has a call number of:

921
Ru

Read each title: Write 920 for collective biography.
Write 921 for a single biography.
Add the correct letters to complete the call number.

1. _____ *Sports Stars* by Roger Sport.

2. _____ *The Life of General Custer* by Edward Alamo.

3. _____ *Famous Television Stars* by Edward Channel.

4. _____ *The Life of Sitting Bull: A Famous Indian* by A.E. Arrow.

5. _____ *The Life of Mel Blanc: Creator of Buggs Bunny* by Ray Doc.

6. _____ *Famous Americans* by John Note.

7. _____ *Jim Henson and His Life* by James Kermit.

8. _____ *Singers and Dancers* by James Music.

9. _____ *George Washington: His Life* by Eileen Cherry.

10. _____ *Famous Leaders* by John Powers.

If the book is a collective biography write "YES." If it is not a collective biography write "NO."

1. _____ *Plays* by Peter Act.

2. _____ *Hamsters and Gerbils and Mice* by Arthur Tail.

3. _____ *Hockey Stars* by Roger Stick.

4. _____ *Famous Explorers* by James Ship.

BIOGRAPHIES—COLLECTIVE BIOGRAPHIES

Collective biography is a book about more than one person. It's call number is 920. The first two letters of the writer's last name follow the number.

Example: *All About Sports Stars* by James Ta has a call number of:

> 920
> Ta

Biographies are books about one person. It's call number is 921. The first two letters of the last name of the person the book is about follow the number.

Example: *All About Sugar Ray Leonard* by Jay Tay has a call number of:

> 921
> Ta

Read each title: Write 920 for collective biography.
  Write 921 for a single biography.
  Add the correct letters to complete the call number.

1. _____ *All About Beverly Cleary* by James Tay.

2. _____ *Famous Writers* by Ronald Smith.

3. _____ *Famous Explorers* by Captain Hook.

4. _____ *Famous Hockey Stars* by Terrence Hall.

5. _____ *George Washington* by Mary Tall.

6. _____ *Story of Sir Francis Drake* by John Poll.

7. _____ *All American Rock Stars* by John Drum.

8. _____ *Movie Stars: Their Stories* by Barbara Star.

9. _____ *Story of Helen Keller* by Ray Stevens.

10. _____ *Story of Captain Hook* by Elizabeth Cole.

If the book is a biography write "YES." If it is not a biography write "NO."

1. _____ *Famous Battles* by J.J. Boom.

2. _____ *Stories About Puppies* by J.J. Dog.

3. _____ *Famous Skaters* by Peter Ice.

4. _____ *Singers: Their Stories* by Sheila Song.

5. _____ *The Presidents* by Craig T. Note.

OVERVIEW—BIOGRAPHIES

Write call numbers for each **biography**.

1. _____ *Benjamin Franklin* by Arthur American.

2. _____ *Thomas Jefferson* by Peter Note.

3. _____ *George Washington* by James Peterson.

4. _____ *John F. Kennedy* by Roger Press.

5. _____ *Walt Disney: His Life* by Linda Cartoon.

6. _____ *Dr. Seuss and His Life* by Alice Kids.

7. _____ *Dolly Madison* by Richard American.

8. _____ *Betsy Ross* by Jenine Flagg.

9. _____ *Helen Keller: A Brave Life* by Helen Strong.

10. _____ *Pocahantas: Her Story* by Joyce Indian.

Write call numbers for each **collective biography**.

1. _____ *Famous Movie Stars* by Evelyn Starr.

2. _____ *Sport Stars in the Eighties* by B. Ball.

3. _____ *Presidents in American History* by Peter Press.

4. _____ *Writers in America* by Peter Paper.

5. _____ *Famous Singing Stars* by James Note.

Is it a biography? (Write yes or no.)

1. _____ *The Lives of the Presidents.*

2. _____ *Dogs and Kittens.*

3. _____ *Walt Disney: His Story.*

4. _____ *Famous Sport Stars.*

5. _____ *Famous Movie Stars.*

A BIOGRAPHY ABOUT _____

WRITTEN BY _____

_____

_____

_____

_____

_____

_____

_____

_____

_____

_____

_____

_____

_____

_____

_____

_____

_____

_____

_____

_____

HAIKU POETRY

The *haiku* is a type of nature poem that first originated in Japan. The haiku always has the same form:

- The first line has five syllables.

- The second line has seven syllables.

- The last line has five syllables.

Although this poetry sounds very simple when spoken, the haiku is difficult to write. The haiku speaks meaningful truth and should not be read through quickly.

Here are some good places to find haikus:

Atwood, Ann. *Haiku: The Mood of the Earth.*
Atwood, Ann. *Haiku-Vision: My Own Rhythm.*
Behn, Harry (translated). *More Cricket Songs: Japanese Haiku.*
Caudill, Rebecca. *Wind, Sand and Sky.*
In the Eyes of the Cat: Japanese Haiku for All Seasons.
Lewis, Richard (compiled). *In A Spring Garden.*
Livingston, Myra Cohn. *O Silver of Liver: Together with Other Triolets,*
    Cinquains, Haiku, Verses and a Dash of Poems.
Mizumura, Kazue. *Flower Moon Snow: A Book of Haiku.*
Mizumura, Kazue. *If I Were a Cricket.*

NAME _____

WRITE YOUR OWN HAIKU

Read the following haiku poetry. Notice the first and third lines have five syllables and the middle line has seven syllables. Remember, it is 5 or 7 syllables – not 5 or 7 words. Illustrate your haiku in the box.

Snow, softly, softly
settles at dusk in a dance
of white butterflies.

OEHARU

Clouds of morning mist
float over the summer hills
like a painted dream.

BUSON

—— —— —— —— —— —— ——

—— —— —— —— —— —— —— ——

—— —— —— —— —— —— ——

THE MYTH

Stories that we read can be very different. Long ago, sometimes, people told stories for a reason. They told stories to explain things. They did not know why these things happened. They did not understand many things. Some things that happened would surprise people. Some things that happened frightened them.

Just think how you would feel if you did not know why some of these things happened. It rains. It thunders. The sun goes down. Long ago, these things were misunderstood. People made up stories to explain these things. These stories made people feel better. These stories are called *myths*. Myths are stories that somehow or someway explained something.

Today, we read these stories for enjoyment.

The main characters in myths are usually gods, goddesses, heroes, monsters, animals, and humans. These are the three main types of myths:

Creation myths explain how the world began, how people came to be, how the moon and stars got up in the sky. These types of myths explain the beginning of things.

Nature myths explain things like why there are seasons, why animals look the way they do, how mountains and rivers came to be, why there is thunder and lightning, and why the planets move around the sun.

Hero myths do not explain anything, but they show the bravery and strength of a character or how a character is involved with love and death.

Greek myths are the most numerous and well-known myths. The Romans also have many myths, but these are actually just different versions of Greek myths. The Northern peoples of Norway, Greenland, Ireland, England, and Iceland are known for a third collection of myths called Norse myths, which have been found in Iceland.

WHERE DID THE MYTHS COME FROM?

On the map below, locate the three main areas where myths have come from: GREECE, Rome (ITALY) and the northern countries of NORWAY, GREENLAND ICELAND, IRELAND, AND ENGLAND. Color Greece green. Color Rome purple. Color all the northern countries blue. Lable all these places with pencil.

THE MYTH

1. Choose a happening of everyday life. It can be something such as why does it snow, rain, change seasons, change of day to night. Write your own myth. Remember, a myth must answer or explain a life happening.

2. Read a myth. Explain the elements of the story that make it a myth and not some other type of literature.

3. Illustrate the myth that you have read. You can do this in a variety of ways. poster, diagram, postcard, etc.

4. Create a myth postcard. Write a short myth and send it to a group of people to help explain a life happening.

5. It is snowing. Big, fluffy, wet snowflakes are falling. But you are in a strange country. The people in this country have never seen snow! Can you make up a story to explain it? Try!

6. Create a book jacket for a myth. A book jacket tells something about the story in pictures and words. Fold a piece of paper in half. Write the title of the story and illustrate your book jacket.

Some myths you can share with the class:

Apollo and Diana
Arcas and Callisto
Atlanta and Hippomenes
Circe and Ulysses
Cupid and Apollo
Cupid and Psyche
Daedalus and Icarus
The Golden Touch
Hercules
Jason and the Golden Fleece
Orpheus and Eurydice
Pegasus and Bellerophon
Perseus and Andromeda
Phaeton and the Chariot of the Sun
Pomona and Vertumnus
Prometheus and the Fire of the Gods
Prosperpina and Pluto
Pygmalion and Galatea
Romulus and Remus

GREEK MYTH MATCHING

Below are nine famous characters from Greek myths. Match each character
on the left to its description on the right.

Apollo	Messenger of the Gods
Zeus	God of the Underworld
Poseidon	God of Light, Truth, The Sun
Hades	Goddess of Wisdom
Athena	Supreme Ruler, Lord of the Sky
Eros	God of the Sea
Persephone	Goddess of Love and Beauty
Hermes	God of Love
Aphrodite	Maiden of Spring

NAME _____

MYTH CHARACTERS

Pick a famous character from a Greek, Roman, or Norse myth and write a short paragraph about him or her. Draw this character below from a scene in the myth.

_____

_____

_____

_____

_____

_____

_____

_____

GHOST STORY

The ghost story is a special type of story that many people enjoy. Ghost stories are enjoyable because they make you sit on the edge of your seat, they are suspenseful. Strange things can happen that do not happen in realistic stories. Usually we are either surprised or scared before a ghost story is over.

A ghost story is really a fantasy story. The story is not real. Characters, happenings, and things do not have to be real. And there is usually something that happens in the story that can not be easily explained. The events can be connected to the supernatural. The supernatural is a word we use for events or characters that are outside the everyday or natural world we know.

The ending of a ghost story does not always tie all the parts of the story together. It can, but often the reader may be left wondering about the ending of the story. Let's look at a typical ghost story with a surprise ending.

Here is a list of ghost stories for you to choose from:

Ainsworth, Ruth. *The Phantom Carousel and Other Ghostly Tales.*

Cohen, Daniel. *Phone Call from a Ghost: Strange Tales from Modern America.*

Corbett, Scott. *The Red Room Riddle.*

Galdone, Joanna. *The Tailypo: A Ghost Story.*

Hancock, Sibyl. *Esteban and the Ghost.*

Harper, Wilhelmina. *Ghosts and Goblins: Stories for Halloween.*

Hopkins, Lee Bennett. *A-Haunting We Will Go.*

Leach, Maria. *Whistle in the Graveyard: Folktales to Chill Your Bones.*

Leach, Maria. *The Thing at the Foot of the Bed.*

Lindgren, Astrid. *The Ghost of Skinny Jack.*

Schwartz, Alvin. *Scary Stories to Tell in the Dark.*

Simon, Seymour. *Ghost*

GHOST STORY ACTIVITY PAGE

1. You open your back door. It's night. It's quiet. You have a strange feeling. Suddenly, a strange shadow pops out from behind the tree. Finish the story.

2. Illustrate your ghost story.

3. Read a ghost story to the class. Have the children rewrite the ending. Remember, a ghost story does not have to have a clear-cut ending. You can leave the readers uncertain about what happens and why. Have the children share their new endings. Compare how many children had similar ideas.

NAME _____

FAVORITE GHOST STORIES

Read a collection of ghost stories from the library. Illustrate scenes from your three favorite stories in the collection.

Title of collection: _____

Author, Editor, or Compiler: _____

Title of story: _____

Title of story: _____

Title of story: _____

Title of story: _____

MY OWN GHOST STORY

_____

_____

_____

_____

_____

_____

_____

_____

_____

_____

_____

_____

_____

_____

_____

_____

_____

_____

_____

Use the following page to illustrate your ghost story.

NAME _____

CAN YOU FINISH THIS STORY ROAD?
Write the title of the books you've read along the story road.

I LOVE TO READ!

1. My favorite book that I've read to myself:

_____

2. The best book that has been read to me:

_____

3. The funniest story I know:

_____

4. The book character that I like best:

_____

5. The most exciting story I have read:

_____

6. The book family I would most like to meet:

_____

7. My favorite animal story:

_____

8. The saddest happening in my books:

_____

9. The author I would most like to meet:

_____

10. I wish we had more books about:

_____

KEEP A RECORD OF YOUR READING

Title	Author	Kind	Like it?

NAME _____

MY BOOK REPORT

The title of the book I read is: _____

Written by: _____

This story was about: _____

_____

_____

_____

_____

I enjoyed this book because: _____

_____

_____

_____

_____

_____

_____

I would tell my friends to read this book because: _____

_____

_____

_____

_____

FOURTH GRADE READING AWARDS

FOURTH GRADE BOOKMARKS

Reading lets you travel to any place in the world!

4th Graders

Love To Read!

INVESTIGATE YOUR LIBRARY

SUGGESTED AUTHORS FOR FOURTH GRADE

ANIMALS
Howe, James
Seldon, George
Sharp, Margery
White, E.B.

BIOGRAPHY
Millender, Dharathula
Stevenson, Augusta
Weil, Ann

FICTION
Blume, Judy
Byars, Betsy
Dahl, Roald
Hurwitz, Johanna

HISTORICAL FICTION
Fritz, Jean
Tripp, V.

MYSTERY
Schultz, Irene
Sobol, Donald J.

SCIENCE FICTION
Slote, Alfred

SCHOOL STORIES
Gilson, Jamie
Kline, Suzy
Peck, Robert
Sachar, Louis

SPORTS
Christopher, Matt

Glossary

autobiography—a book that tells about the life of a person. It is written by the person him/herself.

bibliography—a list of books in alphabetical order by the author's last name. The books are grouped by subject.

biography—a book that tells about the life of a person.

call number—the number under which you will find a book.

book index—an alphabetized list of subjects discussed in the book.

catalog cards (author)—a card whose first line is the author's last name. It gives this basic information about the book: author's name, book title, book description, publisher, place of publication, copyright date, number of pages, and illustrations.

catalog cards (title)—a card whose first line is the title. It gives this basic information: book title, author's name, book description, publisher, place of publication, copyright date, number of pages, and illustrations.

catalog cards (subject)—a card whose first line is the subject. It gives this basic information: subject, author's name, book title, book description, publisher, place of publication, copyright date, number of pages, and illustrations.

collective biography—a book that tells about the lives of more than one person.

Dewey Decimal System—a method of arranging books created by Melvil Dewey. This system arranges books in ten divisions.

encyclopedia cross-reference—a list of other or related topics that you may check to find additional information. Cross-references are found at the end of the article.

encyclopedia headings—a list of topics much like chapters in a book. They divide the encyclopedia article into sections.

encyclopedia index—a list (alphabetized) of topics discussed in the encyclopedia.

encyclopedia subheadings—a list of topics much like chapters in a book. They divide the encyclopedia article into sections.

fiction—a story that tells of people, places, or things that are not real.

fantasy—a fiction story that creates a world where characters, things, or places are not explained.

ghost story—a type of fantasy story that deals with the supernatural.

magazine—a periodical (reading material that is published monthly or bi-monthly.) It contains short articles.

nonfiction—reading material that is based upon fact.

play—a story told by characters. The story is told by acts and in dialogue.

table of contents—a list of articles and their writers and the page numbers that you will find them on.

NOTES